one good thing

Also by M.A.C. Farrant

Short Fiction

Altered Statements
*The Breakdown So Far**
*Darwin Alone in the Universe**
*The Days: Forecasts, Warnings, Advice**
*Down the Road to Eternity: New and Selected Fiction**
Girls Around the House
*The Great Happiness: Stories and Comics**
Raw Material
Sick Pigeon
What's True, Darling
Word of Mouth
*The World Afloat: Miniatures**

Novel

*The Strange Truth About Us: A Novel of Absence**

Non-Fiction

My Turquoise Years
The Secret Lives of Litterbugs and Other True Stories

Plays

My Turquoise Years
Rob's Guns & Ammo

*Available from Talonbooks

one

god

thing

A Living Memoir

BY M.A.C. FARRANT

Talonbooks

Talonbooks
9259 Shaughnessy Street, Vancouver, British Columbia, Canada V6P 6R4
talonbooks.com

Talonbooks is located on xʷməθkʷəẏəm, Sḵwx̱wú7mesh, and səlilwətaʔɬ Lands.

First printing: 2021

Typeset in Minion
Printed and bound in Canada on 100% post-consumer recycled paper

Interior design and cover design and illustration by andrea bennett

Talonbooks acknowledges the financial support of the Canada Council for the Arts, the Government of Canada through the Canada Book Fund, and the Province of British Columbia through the British Columbia Arts Council and the Book Publishing Tax Credit.

LIBRARY AND ARCHIVES CANADA CATALOGUING IN PUBLICATION

Title: One good thing : a living memoir / by M.A.C. Farrant.
Names: Farrant, M. A. C. (Marion Alice Coburn), 1947– author.
Description: Includes bibliographical references.
Identifiers: Canadiana 2020031386X | ISBN 9781772012842 (softcover)
Subjects: LCSH: Farrant, M. A. C. (Marion Alice Coburn), 1947– | LCSH: Chesnut, Helen. Newspaper columns. Selections. | CSH: Authors, Canadian (English)—20th century—Biography. | LCSH: Gardening. | LCGFT: Autobiographies.
Classification: LCC PS8561.A76 Z46 2021 | DDC C813/.54—dc23

For Flynne & Gale

If you want to talk about love, why not begin
with those marigolds you forgot to water?

—**Tony Hoagland**
Priest Turned Therapist Treats
Fear of God (2019)

CUCUMBER

Dear Helen Chesnut,

You have been writing your gardening columns for many years now, but it is only recently that I've begun reading them. As you know, they appear in our local newspaper, Victoria's *Times Colonist*, in the Home section, on Wednesday and Saturday of each week. I used to pass them over because I didn't consider myself a gardener, ignoring them in the same way I still ignore the automotive section and TV listings that appear daily, and the ponderous advice given to strata owners that also appears on Wednesdays.

But now I've suddenly become beguiled by what you write – you offer so many metaphors with which to frame one's thoughts.

You are clearly carrying on a tradition with your column – I believe your father wrote it before you. I hope there'll be a family member to eventually take over from you and follow your example of calm abidance. It's a quality many of us could use just now, and it's one you seem to have in spades – pardon the pun – and have been practising for years. I'm beginning to imagine you as a kind of gardening Bodhisattva: someone who is steadfast, playful, and wise as you continue on your gardening way. Season after season, you have prevailed – planning, working the soil, planting, harvesting, head down, tending your vegetable plot, or with your nose in a flower, but absorbed by the task at hand, then writing about it with care. And all the while the world continues on its own perilous way.

For some strange reason, your column today about growing a memorable cucumber helped assuage my fears about the state of the world. I read it like a psalm. It calmed me way down.

Perhaps it was the optimistic headline – "Seedy Connections Yield Refreshing Results" – that drew me in, and the focus you applied to producing one good thing: a cucumber. I read the column as if it were a life raft of hope.

One good thing.

Planting success, you write, comes from saving seeds from season to season. Seeds are a kind of life raft too, aren't they? Promising continuance, promising the future. And isn't that what a gardener is? A futurist who believes passionately in tomorrow?

This is what I am thinking: What if we could get the same results from seeding hope as you've achieved with seeding the Crystal Apple cucumber? What if we could make hope in these times grow as abundant and refreshing and cooling and prevailing as that cucumber?

I will read your columns in future with this question in mind.

OPEN TRUNK

Dear Helen,

(May I call you Helen? If I'm going to be writing to you in the days ahead?)

I'm always trying to keep the area around my "trunk" open, as you suggest in your column this morning. Or, to put it another way, to receive with openness whatever comes my way. I appreciate your reminder to do this. Again, your column today strikes me as a metaphor.

You say it's not a good idea to have the trunk area so cluttered that fresh air and sunshine can't penetrate to the roots. In fact, that it's crucial to keep the trunk clear. Otherwise you get pests, disease, and weeping dieback. Yes, *weeping dieback*. You say that. The image takes my breath away.

And it's a relief not to be told to take supplements or breathe deeply or think positively if I want to avoid these things. All I have to do is get down to work, clear the trunk, think about something else. It's what Elsie, the aunt who raised me, used to say of my childhood moodiness: "Go down to the beach and play in the seaweed, for heaven's sake! Take your mind off yourself!"

So what I did this morning was take a walk.

I did this after breakfast. Everyone had gone home and, with them, the cars, the dogs, the dramas, the dinners. The three-day holiday was over. I walked out the front door and kept walking for an hour. Initially, the area around my trunk – my body, my state of mind – was difficult to navigate because of all that had occurred during the previous week still adhering to me. Besides the visitors, there had been the bat the cat brought in, which meant the involvement of several government departments, vet visits, rabies shots, and medium-level agitation. (Never, if I may say so, pick up a bat, alive or dead, with a Kleenex – use thick gloves.)

I persisted with my walk and was rewarded with the space around me opening up. For example, the sky appeared. I actually saw it. It was a faded blue, yet still hanging over us in spite of the darkening times.

I also noticed a smiling woman on a bike, several "Robinia Frisia" trees with their bright yellow leaves, a bifold door placed at the end of a driveway with a sign that read "Free," and a lot of Queen Anne's Lace in the ditches.

When I returned home, the house around me was peaceful. The silence I experienced there did not exclude the sound of the birds chirping at the deck feeder, or the engine of the blue-and-white recycling truck out on the street keeping us virtuous.

THE SMALL-SPACE

Dear Helen,

I read your headline today – "A Satisfying Experiment in Small-Space" – as a confirmation, another metaphor in your column that I can appreciate. It was as if you were speaking directly to me. Experimenting with a "small space" is what I've been doing in my writing for years. Satisfaction, at times, is what I've achieved. *Your* small-space, with that hyphen, is none other than my blank white page and the writing I strive to lay upon it. The experiment is the art. It's the small space where ideas and images can shimmer and expand towards the margins.

And, as you say, it's the place where *yield* happens – the place of harvest, but also of surrender, a place to succumb. Yield, with its "usual mix of successes and disappointments, surprises and things learned," you write.

The small-space is life condensed, enlarging when we pay attention to what it can produce.

You speak of gardeners "playing with space." That's it, exactly. It's what writers and poets do with words. What musicians do with notes. Dancers with their bodies. We play, and in doing so find joy in the unfolding world.

So, I welcome your hands-on instructions for maintaining yield in the small-space, and offer my take on it in return. Keeping the soul uplifted is one way to do this. Companion seeding, such as an appreciation of family and of the everyday, is another. The small-space is ultimately our bodies, containing the only life we will ever have, so it's wise to treat it well.

You must have read Lu You, the Chinese poet. He wrote the definitive book about the cultivation and preparation of tea, *The Classic of Tea.*

I am sure he was speaking of the small-space, and how it can enlarge our experience, when he wrote:

> *The clouds above us join and separate,*
> *The breeze in the courtyard leaves and returns.*
> *Life is like that, so why not relax?*
> *Who can stop us from celebrating?*

POWDERY MILDEW

Dear Helen,

A teenager in England, who refused to eat anything but French fries, Pringles potato chips, white bread, and the occasional slice of ham, has gone blind because of his diet. We're told this in today's newspaper as a warning. It reads like a cautionary fairy tale or a myth.

In another section of the paper, we're told that long-running discharge – not from the blind teenager, but from anywhere on our own bodies – needs to be checked, and soon.

There's also advice from a pop singer who says he's sorry for using drugs: "When the odds are against you, keep fighting."

Against corrupt leaders, who are also greedy morons, I want to add. They continue their assault on the vulnerable, which includes the rest of us – the destruction of everyone's ego-system continues apace.

Today's paper seems to suggest we're experiencing the disease at the end of civilization.

Thank goodness that you, Helen Chestnut, have a plan to rehabilitate a world stricken with this disease, which, in your gardening parlance, takes the form of eradicating powdery mildew. Get into the garden and clean up and clear out, you say. Plan for next season!

Because I'm in turmoil about the times we are living through, I'm needing more and more of the calm abidance that emanates from your columns. I've practised yoga for several years. You'd think I'd have been more equipped to find it by now.

SHORT PLOT

Dear Helen,

I am hoping to overwinter. I will do this by listening carefully to everything you say during the months ahead. Overwintering can be about finding solutions to common problems, as you note in today's column about the short plot. It will also constitute my attempt to come to terms with the dual realities – the everyday and the global – that have preoccupied me so much of late.

Your statement that a short plot is worth the effort again sounds like a metaphor to me – keeping things contained and manageable. Because my short plots – my writing about the nature of our lives – are tucked into a corner of last year, and the years before that. They continue to write themselves, and I continue to try and follow where they are going. But it's hard sometimes!

I'm taking heart, though, or maybe I'm trying not to *lose* heart. Overwintering with you will be restorative, I think.

The short plot is really a big opening for the way good things can be seeded forward – like vegetables and love. And any life is a big memoir, if you think about it. Norwegian writer Karl Ove Knausgård tapped into this truth in his series of "novels" titled *My Struggle*. But it's all of our struggles, isn't it? Seasonal short struggles, and rosary bits of joy along the way.

People are getting ready to abandon the conversation; this is becoming clear to me. It's too hard to hold all the threads together: the climate, the refugees, the wars, the diseases, the songbirds' extinction. It's hard to get us to abandon old reasons for the way we've been living. And change is coming too changeably fast. We don't know where the adze will fall next.

I'm not a natural gardener, though I could learn. Focus and patience are required, I think. My plan is to overwinter with you for a season, at least. Perhaps this conversation will flow into spring and summer, as well.

THE FAR END

Dear Helen,

Today's column – "Tomatoes Turn Red at Far End" – gave me a thrill. I have wondered for most of my adult life where *the far end* is. Does your headline mean you know its exact location? Humankind has been asking this question for millennia.

Is death the far end? Or a portal into another dimension? Is it a relative term for where we personally reside on the space-time continuum, the one that stretches from our births to our deaths? Is there a longer far end, that we see in childhood, versus a nearer far end, that we see in old age?

You use the term with such authority, saying, "The far end is the blossom end." But isn't the blossom end the beginning of things?

Your answer to A.M., who asks this question of you, was a little disappointing for a person looking for existential certainty. "Tomatoes are green at the far end, and as they ripen, that part turns red." That's it. That's your explanation, your metaphysics. One sentence. It's not even a haiku. I don't mean to criticize, but it's just that I get testy when the revelations I'd hoped for don't appear. Yes, it's a failing on my part, I know.

You move on from the above explanation about ripening tomatoes to answering C.H.'s question about tan spots on the lawn, and then to K.M.'s question about preventing racoons from digging over two dozen holes in the lawn during the night.

My best guess about the holes in the lawn is that racoons are looking for their own far end, which is down some hole or other. This has always been my understanding about where the far end is.

I wonder, though.

Why am I looking for divination in a column about tomatoes?

SUNSCALD

Dear Helen,

You use the word "sunscald" in your headline this morning. I have never encountered that word before. You mention it in relation to yellow burn marks on ripening tomatoes caused by overexposure to the sun.

Overexposure has been a problem for me this week. I've been feeling burned, yes, scalded, by taking in too much news. One such piece was the essay Jonathan Franzen published in the *New Yorker* titled "What If We Stopped Pretending?" in which he says the climate apocalypse is coming and that our current attempts at climate correction are misplaced and hopeless. "Voting for Green candidates, riding a bicycle to work, avoiding air travel." These things, he says, are not going to stop the catastrophe; it's time we woke up, accepted the fact, and started preparing.

My reaction was to fall into helplessness, fear, and a mad desire to hold on to the sweet state of "pretending" Franzen was warning us against. Then I realized this level of disturbance

couldn't go on and put myself on a regime that included cur-
tailing my exposure to the news, then doing something other
than reacting to it.

I went into the yard. Once there, amidst the silence and the
space, I raked the cut blackberry vines from the side of the yard,
along with the dead laurel leaves, into a satisfying pile. Raked
the pine cones from the driveway. Raked the gravel driveway
itself like a Zen adept.

It's been an odd summer, as you note at the end of today's
column. I agree.

TOAST

Dear Helen,

I was cheered to see you've included a few short recipes in another of your tomato columns this morning. I read that as a tiny bit of encouragement. Eating tomatoes is something I can manage, but the tomatoes are usually grown by someone else because we – Terry and I – have a poor track record when it comes to growing anything. Other than garlic, Mac apples, ever-bearing strawberries that only need water, and blackberries, which need absolutely nothing, we've had little success growing fruits and vegetables, and, in particular, growing tomatoes.

You've been writing a lot about them lately, haven't you? Not that I'm complaining. But your mention of having an overabundance of them, and hence offering tomato recipes – uncooked pasta sauce, salads with bocconcini, and so on – left me feeling dismayed.

Why? Because this year we harvested three tomatoes. That's right: three. They are the black variety, and not pretty to look at. We grew them in the fenced area outside the greenhouse and by some miracle nothing ate them before we could: not deer, rabbits, racoons, or rats. There are three more of them ripening on the vine, which is mildly exciting. If they actually ripen, that will make a six-tomato harvest for us in total.

Terry and I shared the largest tomato yesterday and had it on toast with mayonnaise, salt, and pepper, for lunch. It was really good! "Wow," we said, "this is amazing!"

Last year I planted three magnificent tomato plants in large black pots on the deck. I thought I'd foil the predators by planting them there. The plants were the paste variety and at first they grew well, that is, they became tall and vigorous looking. There were those tiny yellow flowers to keep hopeful about.

Disappointment set when the tomatoes ripened and I began harvesting. For starters, there weren't many of them to harvest. Of those that ripened, the skins were tough and got stuck in our teeth. Their flesh was dry.

But I had enough to make and freeze a medium-sized plastic container of salsa, which I planned to produce for my family at Christmas. But that didn't happen because the container shattered in the freezer. This must have occurred when I thoughtlessly threw the frozen turkey in there. I was afraid of serving plastic shards along with the salsa, so I threw it out.

You can see what I'm up against.

WHEN I PRAISED HIS TOMATOES

A story for you, Helen:

Since they have been taking up a lot of your column space these past weeks, this story is about tomatoes. It's also about love and dedication and goodness of heart, qualities, I suspect, that most gardeners would need to possess.

Because I decided not to try and fail to grow vegetables this year (other than our six tomatoes), I've been buying all the produce I need from a stand up the road – more tomatoes, green beans, corn, chard, cucumbers, the most delicious cantaloupes, carrots, broccoli.

I buy them from Brett, a small farmer. Small in the sense that he farms a small area of two acres and sells what he grows. He has several varieties of tomato, but I like his juicy field tomatoes the best.

When I recently praised them, he said he'd picked them the night before. At 2 a.m. in the morning, after getting his dad back to bed. He said there was still a moon out, and that, although the tomatoes looked black in the faint light, he could tell by the feel of them if they were ripe. He said he saw a meteor shower while he was out there and had paused for a few moments to watch it.

Every night, he told me, he's up with his dad, three or four times. There's just the two of them in the big house. His dad wanders – he's ninety years old.

Brett says he doesn't sleep much these days, because now that it's summer the plants are producing, and there's picking, weighing, and pricing to do. And, of course, there's his dad. "I've aged a lot this past year," he said.

A care worker comes in twice a day to get their meals for them, and to tidy up. Afterwards, his dad will settle for an hour – an hour and a half if Brett is lucky. That's when he gets some time to himself.

His father has vascular dementia and other things. He was once the local district's school superintendent. A few days ago, in a moment of lucidity, he asked his son, "I'm alive, right?"Brett didn't say anything. They both laughed.

"Enjoy the tomatoes," Brett said, as I was leaving. "Safe home."

"It's what the Irish say," he said. "It's what my grandfather said. He was the kindest of men – like my dad."

PEAS

Dear Helen,

If I try to grow peas again, they just might flourish. I'm thinking this because I've been reading the advice you give in this morning's column. The secret, you say, is to grow peas in an outside *sheltered* location.

I emphasize "sheltered" because it seems obvious now. After years of planting peas against the open north-facing greenhouse wall, and watching them produce only a few flowers each spring, I was beginning to wonder at my persistence. It's like the goldfish swimming past the plastic castle in his bowl and saying each time, "Oh what a lovely castle!" The goldfish and I seem never to learn or remember. We are fated to repeat our delusions and mistakes. Why is that, I wonder?

The peas I'm mentioning here are sweet peas. The ones we've had have been like our tomato crop – few. Not enough for a heady bouquet on the coffee table. More like five sprigs in a tiny vase by the kitchen sink.

I am not a natural gardener. I am not a natural pruner. I am not a natural composter.

What I am natural at is appreciation. I appreciate anyone who has the ability to grow a robust garden. And I appreciate your columns, Helen Chesnut. Today, you mentioned sitting on a chair beside your garden shed and basking in the sun while resting from your labours. I can do that. Basking in the sun is something I do well.

I'm a good cleaner-upper, too, which is why I like fall so much. One of my great pleasures is raking our long gravel driveway of maple and oak leaves. I might've mentioned that. We have several trees, and each fall I look forward to at least a dozen raking sessions. Perhaps contemplative raking is my special gardening skill.

ORNAMENTALS

Dear Helen,

Part of the draw about tending a garden must be wanting to stay there and never leaving it. As well, there's the language of flowers to understand, their seasonal blooming and fading, the intense waves of fragrance that some of them have, the joy in beholding their presence.

I've been reading Edith Sitwell's *English Eccentrics.* Her book includes a section called "Ornamental Hermits." These were men who, as living hermits, adorned the gardens of the rich in early-nineteenth-century England. "Adorned" – there is no other word for it. They adorned the garden in the same way a fountain does, or a life-size sculpture of a winged angel.

Wealthy people advertised for "singular and silent" aged persons, who would live for seven years in the provided hermitage – usually a rough hut in a section of the garden. These hermits would wear a sackcloth-type of dress and "under no circumstances must they cut their hair, beard, fingernails or toenails." In exchange for their residence, they would be given food and a small stipend. Guests would then tour the garden and have a look at them. It was an era of viewing "curiosities," of intense interest in the exotic human being. People also toured insane asylums, jails, morgues, peep shows, and visited Barnham and Bailey shows. Titillation and mild shock were the desired effects, as well as gratitude for the spectators' own virtue in belonging to a different, tightly ordered world.

In the turbulent twenty-first century, many of us have an ornamental Buddha in the garden. Why Buddhas? I think because it's a particular cultural expression of "other" and what we, as a culture, seem to be needing just now: a Buddha promises calmness.

The one we have is set on a square of gravel in a semi-enclosed part of the yard. About two feet tall, it is fat and happy. It sits there in all weather. I particularly like to view it in the rain when its weathered concrete surface becomes slicked with leaves.

Besides the Buddha, we have a green, tenpin bowling ball as an "ornamental." Terry found it at a garage sale. The bowling ball is balanced on a two-foot-tall cube of cedar and sits beneath the Mac apple tree. Sometimes deer or a strong wind knock it over, and we'll find it a few feet away. We regard the ball rolling off the cube as one of those random Zen occurrences, so it often stays where it lands for weeks. This is another way of saying that we aren't zealous about the propriety of our yard ornaments.

At our house in Cordova Bay, Elsie had a plastic flower in a small pot on the kitchen table. I suppose it could be called an "ornamental." The red flower, a tulip, was embedded in green cement held in a black pot. It sat on the kitchen table beside the salt-and-pepper shakers for my entire growing-up years.

When the plastic flower got dusty, Elsie washed it in the sink with soap and water. She was careful to keep it out of sunlight so that the red of the flower and the green of its stock wouldn't fade.

Sometimes her husband, my uncle Ernie, balanced his cigarette on the edge of the pot and every time he did, he caught hell.

The only time we had fresh flowers in the house was when my grandmother died – a humble bouquet that was deemed unworthy to place among the grander floral wreaths at the graveside.

WEATHER

Dear Helen,

This day is about clouds – high, streaky cirrus clouds, meaning a change in the weather, the end of summer.

It's about the intimate sex lives of birds, something I'd like to know more about. The pairs that mate for life. We have several pairs of quail that live in the blackberry bushes in the backyard. Do these pairs grow old together, like Terry and I have?

The day is also about my lost spite, and what that might mean. Losing it has brightened everything, and resulted in a kind of refreshing before-and-after story. I thank yoga practice and some special friends for this. Though a heavy black feeling arrived after breakfast. Where did that come from? It was like a sudden squall. I wanted to fall on the bed.

A change in the weather.

Today, I also contemplated my well-loved writing room, the place where I hide my god. As the French poet Paul Valéry advised: "Hide your god, he's your strength." Some would call their god their muse. Occasionally, I join a walking group and secretly take my god with me, imagining all of us pushing our gods – I'm sure others have them, too – in little wheelbarrows trundling down the paths, noticing everything.

During the afternoon there were a few moments of longing when I considered the old Tillicum Drive-In Theatre in Victoria that's now a mall, and how as teenagers we used to – I don't know – go there. A few sentimental details went along with this – losing my bra in a back seat, breaking a tooth on a dry hot-dog bun.

At bedtime, I thought about the elephant, the one who can hear a cry for help in a mote of dust. The big dear thing. Who said that about the elephant's empathy? Was it me? Was it you?

Was it someone from the poet Charles Simic's "silent laughing chorus," in his memory-erasing white room?

CLOUDS

A confession, Helen:

I don't want to know how the story of our time ends. The unfolding of the story is enough. And, happily, there are days when I am like a series of distant altocumulus clouds, rat-a-tatting across a bright blue sky. These clouds bring a lot of light and beauty into my life.

Each cloud lives for ten minutes. I became fascinated with clouds when I discovered this fact in one of my new favourite books, *The Cloudspotter's Guide* by Gavin Pretor-Pinney. I also learned that the average cumulus cloud weighs as much as eighty elephants. How is that measured? I have no idea, but it has to do with a cloud being composed of condensed water vapour. Clouds are not lighter than air, but stay afloat because of convection currents from the sun-warmed ground.

Soon after reading the book, I became a member of the Cloud Appreciation Society, which is based in England and has a worldwide membership. I'm member #23,325 and joined in July 2013. Aside from political parties and writers' associations, this is the only formal organization I have ever belonged to. Membership comes with a certificate and a lapel pin with the word "Cloudspotter" draped around a white cumulus cloud. I wear the pin to literary events.

But to continue. A cloud is always changing. It keeps the form we see when we glance at it for only ten minutes. After that time, the cloud dissolves and assumes another shape, though sometimes it disappears altogether.

For example, a cloud shaped like a terrier with its mouth open – I saw one over the Victoria airport lands recently – may float across the sky towards a stick on the far side of an adjacent cloud. It's a slow process, taking mere minutes. By the time it reaches the stick, the terrier has transformed into something else, a flying saucer, or a rustle of running nuns, and the stick has disappeared.

As a gardener, Helen, I often picture you looking at the sky for information that will tell you when to plant, and how soon, or how late, and whether rain is coming? In this regard, you are very much like my father. His specialty, as a deep-sea master mariner and navigator, was manoeuvring around obstacles – the sudden storms, the change of currents, engine problems, the deadlines for delivering cargo. He could read the sky, the wind; knew rain, fog, clouds, air pressure; and could tell what weather was coming by smelling the breeze. Like him, you must be adept at many of these things.

My own effort currently goes into optimizing the experience of ten minutes of time, whatever shape it takes, and in maintaining a steady attention there, though this is not always an easy thing to do. So, I don't want to know how the story ends.

Not that you are suggesting it. It's just that sometimes – can I say this? – it feels like the only place I'm safe is inside my own life. It's become a kind of holy task to stay there.

EARLY PLANTING

Dear Helen,

Your column today is about the early planting of garlic. Early planting, you say – mid-September to mid-October – is the best way to guarantee large bulbs for next year's harvest.

This got me thinking about my own "early planting" because I often wonder if I've turned out all right – flourished, been "large" enough – considering the shaky start I had. It also got me thinking about my paternal grandfather, who, by the family's estimation, didn't flourish at all.

A favourite saying of my father's was "Steady as she goes," meaning you set your course and move steadily towards it – which is much like your advice about planting garlic.

But my father, Billy, after being married for a short time, had to change his course and, because his new course didn't include Nancy, my mother, he became a single father, albeit from a distance in Vancouver, where he worked on the docks supervising the loading of cargo ships.

Nancy, like a perfect storm, appeared only a few times in my early life and, when I turned five, she fled home to Australia for good. I saw her only once after that, when I was seventeen. She arrived in Vancouver for an overnight stay on the cruise ship *Canberra* with her fifth husband, Stanley. I visited her onboard. She had little to say to me, and fell asleep in her chair during my visit. I quickly left, thinking how lucky I was to have escaped her.

Her stand-in during my formative years in Victoria was my father's older sister, Elsie, who was forty-seven years old when she took me on. Elsie was a no-nonsense but very engaged handler. She could sew anything, knit anything, handle anything, including me, because I was something of a wild girl when she got me – undisciplined, wilful, angry. The large extended family included her oppressed second husband, Ernie, the janitor at the Victoria Public Library; her daughters, Doreen and Shirley, who were fourteen and ten years older than me; her older sister, Maudie, a gentle widow, who made my dolls' clothes – knitted sweaters, lace-trimmed underpants – and Grandma, my father's mother, who had only one hand – her left – because her right hand was cut off after a break that didn't heal properly. Grandma covered the stump with a grey sock held in place by a red elastic band. She lived with Maudie.

My grandfather died before I was born. He was remembered as a barber and a drunk. The drunk part was why Grandma in her dementia would pour anyone's drink down the sink one-handed – beer, rye, apple juice, milk, tea – you had to watch her; she moved fast.

No one, it was said, was surprised when my grandfather died of cirrhosis of the liver at sixty-two. There are few stories about him – "Grandpa Gibson," he was called, or "Pa." We knew he grew up in an orphanage in Dublin, then moved to Liverpool, England, and became a barber and had his own shop. But he'd go off on binges for days on end, leaving Grandma and six kids eating sheep's brain soup. That soup was a feature in the telling. It was his fault everyone in the family was short, Elsie said, because they didn't get proper nutrition in England. They had to eat that horrible soup.

Grandpa drank the grocery money, the rent money, and most of what he made as a barber. This is the sum of the stories. The family emigrated to Canada in 1920, to Victoria, on Vancouver Island. My grandmother had two brothers in the poultry business there and I suppose the thinking was that her husband could be a barber and perhaps reform. Not to be. During the sea voyage over, he was either drunk and playing cards, or just plain drunk. The years in Canada were to be the same.

Eric Idle, of the Monty Python troupe, has said that anyone abandoned by their mother becomes a comedian. He also grew up in an orphanage, and so what seems true for Eric Idle about being a comedian is also true for me. Because early on I learned I could make people laugh by putting on skits, using parody, and memorizing the longest words in the dictionary to confound and delight them. But being a comedian was not something that was said of my grandfather, James Joseph. He was always described as a cranky man, and not much fun. There's only one informal picture of him. It shows a short, slight man standing in front of a fence, with sparse hair, thin face, sunken eyes. He looks like Samuel Beckett.

Having a drunk as a father was no doubt why Elsie had such a low opinion of men, including Ernie. "They're all alike," she'd declare. "Useless. Every damned last one of them." The effects of alcoholism travel the generations, and because of this, all six of my grandparents' children, as well as *their* children, were or are sober, dutiful citizens keeping tightly to "me and mine," meaning themselves.

The Gibson family's address in Liverpool was 62 Lodge Lane. Maudie often told stories about living there; you'd think the place was a castle.

Our son, Bill, found the house nearly a century later on a trip to Liverpool to watch the soccer team, Liverpool United. The house was still standing, located in a run-down area beside the railway tracks, and had been converted into slum apartments. There was a fish and chip shop on the ground floor where my grandfather's barbershop had once been. Bill said you wouldn't want to live there.

15

PERENNIALS

Dear Helen,

This day is about the brown-tipped ends of oak leaves signalling the end of summer, dryness in the garden, everything being parched and dusty, and watering the cedar and pine trees in the early morning.

It's about the cats sleeping beneath the antique rose bush. Antique because the rose dates from the early part of the last century. We grew it from a cutting the next-door neighbour gave us. In June, there's a mass of tiny white roses with a strong, sweet scent. The cats sleep under it to keep watch on the fourteen quail that live in the blackberry bushes at the bottom of the yard. The quail always know when the cats are around, keeping one of their kind on watch from the willow tree.

Your column today consists of your answers to two readers' questions. First, W.D. asks if now, being early fall, is a good time to plant perennials. The first part of the headline – "Still a Bit of Time Left" – pretty much answers the question, though I could take that phrase and run with it towards ticking clocks, hourglasses, panic, and old age. But I won't because today I'm feeling like a perennial that is still managing to thrive.

Curiously, and as an aside, W.D. was also my father's initials: William Derbyshire. I was always proud that those letters figured so prominently in his official title: Captain W.D. Gibson, though the family called him Billy, and treated him as something of a small, weak boy. And naive when it came to women. This was Elsie's estimation. "He had no sense at all. That Nancy was a train wreck. After her, forget it!" Captain W.D. was not a perennial when it came to women.

The second question today came from K.M., who asks about poor, dry soils.

Poor, dry soil must be why the trees and bushes we have planted over the years have become large and old. The soil is clay, as is all the native soil in our area of Deep Cove on the Saanich Peninsula, but it does well for the hardier types, the firs, oaks, pines, and maples.

I think we must be hardy, too. Thirty-nine years after building our house, we are still here. Through years of lost jobs and tight money; out-of-control teenagers; writing successes and failures; illnesses; the seventeen years my mother-in-law lived uneasily below us in a suite, and then her dementia. But this is the place where our children grew up, and where one of them was actually conceived. We're still lying in the same bed, still looking at the same whirling stars through the bedroom windows. At night it's so quiet you can hear a dog bark a block away.

It embarrasses our daughter, Anna, to be reminded of where she began, to picture the act of her creation. But imagine visiting the place where you started your miraculous adventure. Wouldn't you want, at the very least, to pause and wonder?

Do you know the exact spot where you began, Helen? I'm tempted to ask if it was somewhere near a garden. I can't say for sure where I began. But it must have been in the southern hemisphere – in Hobart, Tasmania (lutruwita), Nancy's home; in Wellington, New Zealand (Aotearoa), for the marriage; or on Fiji (Viti), for the honeymoon.

I know where I will end, though. On the Saanich Peninsula, outside of Victoria, on Vancouver Island. This is where I put down roots and "stayed put," like all of Elsie's family did. We live fifteen minutes from where I grew up.

16

SHADE-LOVING

Dear Helen,

You now appear to be offering me gardening advice in my dreams. Last night you said: "Cushy-textured, fertile soils can be a problem for this plant, which does well inside the doorway of a bowling alley."

The plant in question was a fern and, in my dream, I was digging it out of a forest. Terry has a dark area beside the house where he grows things that like shade – "shade-loving," as you call it. He's done this for a few years, and some of the plants have actually lived. In the dream, I was thinking of his upcoming birthday and that a new fern might be a good bet as a present.

But the reference to the bowling alley stymied me, even though I found it delightful. There's a bowling alley in Sidney called Miracle Lanes, a name which suggests delight. "Miracles," as the *Merriam-Webster.com Dictionary* defines them – aside from incidences of divine intervention – are an "extremely outstanding or unusual event, thing, or accomplishment." The dictionary gives this sentence as an example: "The bridge is a *miracle* of engineering."

Curious, I visited Miracle Lanes the day after I had this dream. I wanted to see if there was a plant inside the door.

There wasn't – just a vending machine beside the counter, and a notice board with the hours of operation listed. It's a small bowling alley – four lanes – and the game is five-pin, automated, with computer screens above each lane that keep track of the scores.

Helen, did you ever watch *The Big Lebowski*, with the bowling scene of actor John Turturro in purple spandex playing a rival Latino bowler, Jesus Quintana? God, that was fabulous, and funny. That's what I was hoping to find at Miracle Lanes.

Of course, I didn't. What I found there were about a dozen roughhousing teenage boys in jeans and ball caps waiting for their games to begin, each a far remove from the Turturro type. The sole employee, a tall young guy with dreadlocks, jumped in and gave them a "rules of behaviour" talk, and they calmed down.

When the employee returned to his chair and cellphone behind the counter, I asked, "Overall, how's business here?"

"Not great," he said.

I've discovered that an "extremely outstanding event" can happen just about anywhere and at any time – in *The Big Lebowski* – and especially in dreams, the place where phantoms, and other kinds of "shade lovers," routinely dwell.

They can also occur on the streets of Sidney. An event of the outstanding variety happened at the Beacon Café this summer when my friend Josephina passed by as I was having coffee at one of the curbside tables. I call Josephina my guardian angel because she is the first person to ever say she would pray for me, and then things miraculously worked out – "miracle" – that word again. Josephina's a small, middle-aged Portuguese Canadian woman who has raised five children as a single mother, has eleven grandchildren, and is known for the radiance of her personality.

That afternoon she held a boy of ten or so by the hand. He was scowling and dressed entirely in black.

She said, "Let me introduce you to my grandson, Rory. Isn't he beautiful?" She was beaming. "Isn't he the most beautiful boy in the world?"

17

WORMS IN THE ROSES

Dear Helen,

Pests boring into the middle of apples is the subject of today's column, a problem that has arisen in our area over the past couple of years. You write that the pests in question are codling moths, and that they overwinter as larvae at the base of the tree; in the spring, they become adult moths, laying eggs on developing fruit.

The only way to control any and all pests in the garden, you say, is by "sanitation and visual monitoring," that is, by keeping your garden "clean," and by paying attention to everything that is happening there.

This comment about sanitation and vigilance is something I could have used at the outdoor party we attended for our friend Glen's seventy-fifth birthday in May of last year.

The day of the party was overcast, but in late afternoon the sun broke through the clouds. When that happened, all the greenery around us became vibrant, shockingly so. I suddenly noticed the orange poppies, purple foxgloves, and white-flowering cistuses planted here and there, and became aware of their profound and separate existences. It was the same for the swaying fir and alder trees that bordered the property. Everything around us was throbbing with life.

I watched as Melinda took off her shawl and left it on the back of an outdoor chair, then wandered towards Judy, who was standing beside a pink tree peony with a gin and tonic in her hand.

A few of us sat in the more formal area of the garden, chatting. Everyone was waiting for the domed brick oven to heat up so the pizzas could be made. Heather, whose garden this was, had made the oven herself.

I was sitting beside my friend Phil. We were surrounded by the brilliant light and I was feeling a kind of rapture. It occurred to me that sometimes the background takes over, like it was doing then. And when that happens, the self seems to disappear.

I said to Phil: "It's getting harder and harder to reconcile what we are currently viewing – the light, the astounding beauty of the day – with the continual stream of bad news that's forever coming our way, especially the many losses of things – birds, ice, butterflies, trees – and how every loss requires an emotional response, usually one of stunned despair over our impotency to do much about them, and isn't that our culture's dominant mood right now, one of stunned despair?"

"Hmm," he said.

"Despair about the fast and terrible changes that are happening in the world," I said. "It's like we're having to live on two levels – the everyday and the global. When what we really want is to have light-filled afternoons, like today, with a glass of wine in hand and friends to talk to and not this other awareness, the one that darkens joy."

Phil turned and nodded. "Yes," he said. "I see it. What you're describing is like those novels written about the unease people felt before the start of the First World War. The calm, settled lives overshadowed by the possibility of war. Those novels were contemporary then, and almost nostalgic now, playing up the innocence of the times."

"I can't avoid feeling the unease," I said.

"No one can. But people still had parties then, like we do now," he said. "And danced, loved, had children, made music, made gardens, made plans for tomorrow."

It's the beauty of the ordinary, I thought, and felt a sudden longing for the everyday, for its takeover of the global drama.

Phil got up to join Melinda, his wife, and I walked over to join Terry, who was standing with our friends, Patrick and Gail. The three of them were laughing, about what I didn't know, but I wanted some of it.

Later, while everyone was eating pizza, the conversation turned to roses and how they were taking a beating this year. It was a different kind of worm doing the damage, apparently. Such talk, as you'd expect, is something I shy away from because I am beyond the pale when it comes to gardening knowledge.

A group of guests, including me adopting the guise of animated interest, had a look at the six bush roses in the yard. Leaves had been eaten and rosebuds had dropped off. Melinda, a committed gardener, showed us the suspected culprit, a tiny green looper worm. Heather, with her expertise in permaculture, disagreed. She said the culprit was another worm, a small lime-green one. If only I'd known about the importance of sanitation and vigilance then, I could have inserted the concept as a knowing comment.

When it started to rain, we took the food and went inside, where I began chatting with Patrick, who has been an experimental musician for most of his adult life. Our families have been friends for years. An intense gardener, he is forever offering me seeds. I have a drawer filled with them.

Heather came towards us as we were chatting. Her new husband had recently had a stroke and she'd been feeling shaky at the party. But she held out her hand firmly as she approached. It held a tiny lime-green worm. "This is the worm that's been eating the roses," she said.

"Yes, it is," said Patrick with authority.

I nodded my head in agreement.

What else could I do?

18

ABRACADABRA

Dear Helen,

Your column today – "Preparing for the Changing Season" – focused on attending to "troublesome" and "tiresome" parts of the garden, such as broken fencing and out-of-control weeds.

Troublesome and tiresome are good descriptions of my feelings about today's pullout supplement, called "55-Plus," that was slid into the Home section, next to your column. Changing seasons and aging seemed to be the newspaper's special focus today.

The supplement, which was really a sales vehicle for products connected to human aging, contained an article titled "Caregiving 101." It was about Joan, sixty-three, who works three days a week as a live-in to a "senior gentleman" called Mitch, eighty-seven. "We're having an end-of-life blast," says Joan.

Another article was about Harold, who has plantar fasciitis and grave concerns about bunion growth. Always a careful shopper, he likes a crematorium ad that promises "Lowest Price Guaranteed!"

Suggestions for the 55-plus crowd included:

1. If you want a paper route to keep busy, call Tanya at the circulation desk.
2. If you want a walk-in bathtub to stay safe, visit Mason at Bath Emporium.
3. If you want to put your mind at ease about the days ahead, have fun, make a bucket list.
4. If you're worried about your brain, join a Memory PLUS club.
5. If you want information about your golden years, ask your pharmacist. They're here to help.

Ask them how to dodge reality like a matador, I wanted to add, and immediately visited my go-to quote when the inevitable shows its collapsing face:

Give your fire until the last of your days.

It's a translation from the Hebrew of the real meaning of the word "abracadabra," which can be found in the calendar book *Children of the Days: A Calendar of Human History* by Eduardo Galeano under the entry for December 31.

Like me, you probably thought the word was part of a magic trick. As in, "Now you see it, now you don't." As in, a rabbit or a woman is about to disappear.

19

TROPICAL LUXURY

Dear Helen,

I was curious if the word "abracadabra" was attached to anything in the garden and, sure enough, after a Google search, I found the Abracadabra rose, a small, red-and-yellow-striped rose that is not especially beautiful to look at. In fact, it looks overwrought, as if it couldn't decide what to wear to the party, the red or the yellow outfit, and, in desperation, wore them both, their colours clashing horribly.

I was wondering at the odd name of this rose when I began reading your column today. It features a colour picture of a tropical plant that has pointed, waxy green leaves and red flowers, each one looking like a small piece of folded-over paper. The flowers have cream-coloured, wormlike coils attached to them.

Like the mismatched Abracadabra rose, this plant, an anthurium (I will never remember the name), is not lovely to look at. Why would anyone want one, was my first thought? The picture is meant to highlight today's topic, which is bringing "tropical luxury" into your home to brighten up the coming winter.

I'm acquainted with gardeners who love nothing better than being bent-kneed and dirty among their growing things and feel melancholic when their banks of black-eyed Susans, dahlias, zinnias, poppies, petunias, and everything else, find their way to the compost pile. The state of having a bloom-free garden is a tough one for them to handle, hence, probably, their need to bring hothouse exotics inside.

I'm supposing this feeling is behind today's column about brightening up winter. Personally, I have never felt the need to brighten up winter; I like the rain and the dense, low clouds of the Pacific Northwest; I like the feeling of being dormant. Have I been missing something? Winter is when I do most of my writing.

It sounds as if anthuriums are fussy plants. There's much to worry about, as you note – under-watering, overwatering, soil needs, high-humidity needs – so perhaps this worry is their appeal; it's something to keep a gardener active during the winter months. That and reading seed catalogues and planning for spring.

The most I do to cheer up winter is buy a few chrysanthemums at the grocery store because they're worry-free and last a couple of weeks, unlike red tulips that look great for the first day, but whose stems, by the second day, have bent in half and the heads are lying on the dining-room table in some kind of death throe. Why is that?

Questions like this, I suspect, are hooks for the neophyte gardener (I'm resisting saying "budding gardener"). It's the peril of wanting to know things. Once you start asking questions, watch out, your interest will be piqued, and you'll soon be asking *more* questions. Or, like me, composing a letter to Helen Chesnut herself with the question: "Why do store-bought tulips wilt? And what can I do to help them stay erect?"

DAFFODIL BULBS

Dear Helen,

I had a good time in the garden yesterday with a box of daffodil bulbs. The printing on the box said there'd be a minimum of thirty assorted bulbs, but when, two weeks after buying them, I opened the box, I found there were more than eighty bulbs inside. The anxiety over this development was almost too much to handle. Where to put them all?

But I kept thinking how brilliant it would be next March with daffodils blooming in the cold sun and how glad I'd be feeling about that. This thought kept me going: "Look at my daffodils!"

I settled on large pots for the bulbs, and actual dug-up dirt (versus potting soil), something I felt robust about doing with the shovel I found buried beneath some blackberry vines.

Because there were many more bulbs than advertised, and because many of the bulbs crinkled like paper, I worried I was planting duds, that they wouldn't bloom, and that I'd be disappointed again. Was this another example of my gardening excitement outpacing sound judgment? But then, would a bulb company really toss in fifty dead bulbs?

So, I planted. While I worked, the outside air temperature went from warm to cool and back again, depending on the shifting clouds. Because of the recent rains, the dirt was crumbly, like the topping on an apple crisp. Our tortoiseshell cat, Aggie, followed me about and kept me company, rubbing against my bent shoulder as I worked.

This planting with the cat alongside went on for a while, but then I began having a full-body sense of being in direct contact with the experience itself – of entering into the place where nothing else matters except the activity at hand. I've experienced this place often while writing, while giving birth to my children, but never before while working in a garden. And this time it was different because it was also prolonged and included all my senses. A feeling of deep happiness overcame me. Was this the bliss gardeners claim they experience on a regular basis?

Later, I had a look at some gardening quotes that might describe my experience. I found the expected inspirational ones about "pure gladness" (Lillie Langtry); "beauty everywhere" (Vincent Van Gogh, but not, presumably, while he was in that wheat field); "an instrument of grace" (May Sarton); and, "When you stop growing, you start dying." Oh, sorry. That's William S. Burroughs, known more for his literary power and drug use than his gardening skill. He often shows up when I'm writing something, sneering at me in his three-piece suit, smoking his long cigarette. I preferred George Eliot's lighter and more practical advice, and shooed him away. She said: "It will never rain roses. If you want roses, plant rose bushes."

And Gertrude Stein's droll comment. "A vegetable garden in the beginning looks so promising and then after all little by little it grows nothing but vegetables nothing nothing but vegetables."

I know that thought. And her position on commas. She said using them was "pretentious" because they direct the reader when to pause and take a breath in a sentence. "You are always taking a breath," she said, "why emphasize one breath rather than another breath?"

21

SPRUCING UP

Dear Helen,

There are dozens of types of gardens, as I've been learning this morning from the *Encyclopædia Britannica* website – flower, vegetable, woodland, rock, Japanese, water, roof, patio, herb, and so on; and they all have their special "elements" and requirements.

But the encyclopedia didn't mention the instant front gardens that are made by contractors working for real-estate agents. There are many such gardens in our neighbourhood now, seemingly sprung up overnight like mushrooms. You go out for a morning walk, and there's another one.

It's a deeply non-personal look, this instant gardening: bland, clean, and unoffensive, made up of a carpeting of bark mulch, a few large rocks, some tall beige grasses, some small green shrubs. The look is meant to add curbside appeal to the house on offer, make it appear neat and attractive to prospective buyers. It's called "staging" or "sprucing up," to make an impression.

No doubt it's a better look than the "before" appearance of the house – I have one in mind – that featured a chewed-up lawn, dead daisy stalks, overturned bikes, and plastic garbage cans.

My future brother-in-law, Rickey, was a human example of "sprucing up" when he got ready to be best man on the morning of Terry's and my wedding. That is, he had a shower, blow-dried his beard and long hair, and traded his greasy jeans for Terry's leather pants and matching jacket. He went from looking like a guy who lived beneath his truck to looking like a rock-concert producer.

The problem with "sprucing up," though, is that the sprucing must be maintained. Otherwise, "sprucing down" occurs. This was what happened to Rickey after the wedding lunch (it was a tiny, morning wedding) when he spilled red wine in his beard and on the leather pants, which he soon replaced with his beloved jeans.

The same thing – sprucing down – often happens after the house with the instant front-yard treatment is bought and moved into. Before long, weeds appear and flourish, garbage cans reappear, and the new owner's personal stamp becomes evident; they've turned the place into their home. One I noticed recently had added a hydrangea bush, hanging baskets, a wicker chair for the front porch, and a doormat that read, "Oh Shit, Not You Again." I saw it when I was collecting for the Western Canada Wilderness Committee. The fierce woman who answered the door was pushing a walker.

Most everyone keeps the bark mulch from the instant treatments, as had this woman. But it's touch and go whether the grasses and shrubs will make it.

Is the mulch actually made of spruce bark?

22

PERSONAL STRAIN

Dear Helen,

When I saw the words "Personal Strain" in part of your headline today about saving seeds, I thought you'd invented two new words for "stress." "Personal strain" is so much more evocative than "stress." Stress happens to machines and fabric and plants in drought conditions; it's specific; it's about wear and tear. Personal strain happens to our raging hearts, our befuddled brains, our *joie de vivre*. Personal strain is a symphony of woes versus the occasional complaint from a stressed-out string quartet.

I was thinking this when I came across an online article by Anthony Wing Kosner in Dropbox's *Work in Progress* blog – "The Mind at Work: Karl Friston on the Brain's Surprising Energy." It's about the work of neuroscientist Karl Friston and how our brains organize things that happen in the outside world so we can minimize surprise and create predictability in our lives.

How to protect ourselves from the "casual complexity of the world," and from prolonged uncertainty, has been Friston's main area of research. The brain, he says, helps us maintain certainty, and it does so with "surprising energy."

What a time our brains must be having maintaining certainty these days. External events are at a roiling boil, changeable within the hour. There are times when I am going about in a state of despair while trying to maintain this certainty about tomorrow. It often seems an impossible task.

Hence the calm appeal for many, myself included, of Buddhism, Taoism, meditation, yoga, cycling, knitting, raking the driveway; and for others, any number of single-minded pursuits – being a birder, quilter, collector, boater. You ride the calm you gain from these activities through whatever chaos comes hurtling at you. You enter a state of mind in which uncertainty is not a problem because uncertainty is a fact of life; it is our reaction to uncertainty that causes us problems.

In this light, I'm beginning to understand the appeal of gardening. "When you take a flower in your hand and really look at it, it's your world for the moment," Georgia O'Keeffe is quoted as having said years ago when there were other urgent and critical events afoot, but the thought still holds.

Karl Friston has a daily regime to protect himself from prolonged uncertainty. He does this by creating a personal cocoon, which involves sticking to a daily agenda of not speaking to anyone before noon and not participating in social media. His aim is to "minimize the free energy of distractions, complexity, and unavoidable uncertainty" that will rob him of his time doing research, and writing.

Having a personal cocoon in this fashion is an option, I suppose, but it seems restrictive, boxing yourself in, with your eyes tightly shut, and your arms held rigid at your sides, embracing nothing. Yet his manoeuvres to evade "unavoidable uncertainty" are attractive and one good way I've found to do this is to restrict my news intake, the "psychic cancer," as Greg Jackson (writing in *Harper's Magazine*, in an article titled "Vicious Circles: Theses on a Philosophy of News"), brilliantly calls it. "Being fed trivialities when we need importance, like empty calories when we need nourishment, makes us sick."

I'm attracted to blueprints for survival. To-do lists. Steps to climb. Obstacles to overcome. All of these things are weak attempts at controlling chaos, I know, but their requirement of staying focused on one thing helps. I still have (and refer to) *Nuclear War Survival Skills* by Cresson H. Kearny, a detailed manual that was published in 1980 by the Oak Ridge National Laboratory in Tennessee during the "weapons of mass destruction" phase between the Soviet Union and the United States. Terrified by this event, I bought ten copies at the time and gave them to family and friends. The book gave me a sense of certainty about what I could do to protect my family in the aftermath of a nuclear war. I learned how to stockpile food, build a makeshift toilet, detect rates of radiation fallout – the importance of staying underground for at least twenty-four hours and, I've since been told, frighten my children. "This is what we grew up with," they now drolly tell their friends, offering a picture of the book's grim black-and-grey cover as evidence of my questionable parenting skills.

"Yes," I say. "And I grew up beneath the shadow of the atomic bomb. As you know, Hersey's *Hiroshima* has always been mandatory reading on August 6 of each year. Futhermore," I add, quivering, "the Doomsday Clock was created during the year I was born! These are the things *I've* had to live with!"

Driving home from lunch with a friend today, there was some soft guitar music playing on the car radio; melancholic music suggesting a surfeit of personal strain. I listened closely for the title when the music finished. What I heard was "Research on Lost Time" and thought, "What an interesting undertaking that would be, researching the many times in your life when the world *wasn't* yours for the moment." The times, say, when you were robbed of it by anger, needless worry, scrolling on your phone, streaming police dramas, fearing the future.

When I checked the CBC playlist later, the title of the music turned out to be disappointingly Proustian: "In Search of Lost Time" by Jacob Gurevitsch.

23

MORE TOIL THAN JOY

Dear Helen,

A personal gardening cocoon must be maintained, you write in today's column, actually using the word "cocoon," as if you'd just been reading that Karl Friston article. Your column's title was "When Garden Is More Toil than Joy, Time to Simplify."

There are so many nasty things for the gardener to worry over, I took from what you wrote: sap-sucking insects – scales and aphids – and their infestations on hapless hydrangeas was one example. Reading along, it struck me that the amount of knowledge a home gardener must possess is staggering. And scales! I'd never heard of this insect before, an insidious, almost invisible "crawler" that requires a massive amount of work to get rid of, work that includes washing each afflicted leaf with a soft cloth and soapy water and picking the crawlers off with your fingers. If this doesn't work, bring out the insecticidal guns, but only specific, everything-natural guns, with not too much of this or that compound, like a high-school science experiment.

Work such as this would give me a headache, so I'll take your advice to simplify. I'll get rid of all such plants. I'm not made for this kind of toil.

24

VAPOUR BREAKDOWN

Dear Helen,

Looking out the window this afternoon, it struck me that the clouds flying past were like the last sentence of a novel. They were closing the book on what was supposed to be a bright fall day. The thin cirrus clouds were heading east. They looked agitated in their flight, torn apart, as if they were having a special kind of breakdown, a vapour breakdown.

Sure enough, there was a blanket of nimbostratus clouds advancing from the west like a grey phalanx. Soon we'll be enshrouded in rain, and more rain. The garden here, the yard, will become mud. Worms will rise through the grass and dirt to escape their own version of an "extreme weather event," their personal flood. The last geraniums on the deck, the ones that didn't make it into the house this week to overwinter, will probably bloat and die. I should rush outside and save them, I thought. Will I? Helen, you would have been proud. I did!

The novel I had in mind for its last sentence is Kurt Vonnegut's *Hocus Pocus,* an anti-war novel, as are all his novels. An "anti-excrement" novel, he might also have said, as in "after the excrement hit the air-conditioning." This is because "human beings [are] killing the planet with the by-products of their own ingenuity."

Excrement is hitting the fan right now.

The last sentence of Vonnegut's novel is, "Just because some of us can read and write and do a little math, that doesn't mean we deserve to conquer the Universe."

The line underscores today's news, which was about another "worst crisis", another "political con," the ongoing "insanity in high office," another "threatened species," "leaking pipelines," a "worrisome virus," a "threatened war," and "fibre forests," which, I learned, are not really forests at all but huge one-species crops planted on clear-cut land and meant for eventual markets.

God, we are a stupid species.

With the weather and the world the way they are, I can see why gardeners would be cocooning with indoor plants today. Wearing rain gear would not make outdoor gardening a joyous affair. Better to get a soft cloth and warm soapy water and bathe the ornamentals, stay on track for that "world in a moment," which I'm discovering you can get from attending to a plant – any plant.

Or a book, or a keyboard, which is where I'm having my world of moments just now.

Vowing to stay away from the news. It's always break-ing. My heart.

Everyone's heart.

25.

TIME-LAPSE BEES

Another story for you, Helen:

This one is about a film that includes peas, strawberries, and dandelions, and which was made using a time-lapse camera. The presenter told us before the showing that the film's sole purpose was to have us "revel in the beauty of life."

Thirty of us faced the large TV screen on stage at St. John's United Church, here in Deep Cove, and were not disappointed. We showed our appreciation throughout the film by clapping often.

We clapped for the pea pod emerging from its stalk. And for the field of dandelions, first blossoming, then dying back, then sprouting, and blossoming again through the next season.

We thought nothing could be more beautiful than the ripening of a strawberry. And the way night raced over the monuments in our nation's capital, and then it was dawn with swirling clouds.

At one point we clapped for the single plastic bag, which was partially covered by wet leaves. It was lying in a ditch. We watched while it didn't disintegrate, though the leaves around it rotted and disappeared. We clapped because we'd been told that plastic bags in landfills would take a thousand years to disintegrate and here was proof.

We thought the speedy egg and sperm event was funny and laughed outright. And the dozens of honeybees suspended in sunlight was a "living tapestry." This remark was made by a woman in the row ahead of us, Marsha Boon, who sells plants by the side of the road, and whose husband, "Mr. Miracle," as she calls him, had recently died for twenty-seven minutes while watching daytime TV, and was revived by paramedics.

Finally, we clapped for the white-haired man who bowed to us three slow times from the stage when the film he'd presented was over – Peter Roper, who teaches yoga, and organizes the local Heart and Stroke Foundation campaign.

There was a collection basket going around in support of Peter's work, but Terry didn't put his hand in his pocket to contribute. He'd sat beside me in the back row and I don't think he clapped once. When the film ended, he said he hated the way it made time pass so quickly.

"It's bad enough at normal speed," he said. "I don't need to watch time on steroids. That's like watching myself disintegrate."

A squirming two-year-old was being carried out of the hall by her mother, who'd heard Terry's remark.

"Time can't go fast enough for me," she said.

These little towns. Everybody shows up. Everybody has something to say.

26

OUTLAWS

Dear Helen,

"Gardening is an insatiable passion, a bucolic and meditative occupation, yet it wants the vigor and freedom of the forest and the outlaw," wrote Henry David Thoreau in *Walden*, a book published in 1854 about living simply in nature.

Outlaws must have been on your mind, Helen, when writing today's column, because the headline was loud: "Dreaded Hoof Marks in Veggie Patch."

You were referring to southern Vancouver Island's most voracious predator, the free-roaming deer. The subtitle of *Walden* is *Life in the Woods*, something few of us have, our natural habitats being either a city or a suburb. Enter the hapless, overabundant deer. They've become city dwellers and suburbanites alongside us. But it's an uneasy cohabitation.

A large colour picture, which took up a third of your column, showed a doe and two spotted fawns prancing daintily across someone's newly cut lawn, and again I thought of Thoreau sitting serenely on the doorstep of his cottage for an entire day, as he wrote of it, gazing at what was going on outside.

If there had been foraging deer eating Thoreau's lettuce and beans on that memorable day, I wonder if his observation would have been so bucolic. Our own viewing couldn't have been described as bucolic when we caught them eating our rosebuds, tulips, and hosta plants. Terry uses a sling shot and white marbles from the deck to shoo them away, but they rarely shoo; they simply saunter off, as if to say, "Was there something you wanted?"

Most of the time they feed at night, which explains the disappearance this year of the lacecap hydrangea flowers on the bush beside the front door, discovered when I let Aggie out early one morning. The deer had eaten the flowers down to their nubs. My using the word "nubs," by the way, is giving me a thrill; it's newly acquired, one I found in today's column, and doesn't it sound like I know what I'm talking about? Language is everything if you want to speak with authority. Gardening words have been sticking to me like burrs of late.

But, that aside, today's column was timely. The dreaded hoof marks of your headline were none other than those in your own vegetable patch, which the "cheeky" deer had entered, you wrote, from a tiny, open corner of your garden, and there had done their worst. Apparently, they will eat anything if they're hungry enough, even English ivy, and they must have been hungry because we've had a long, dry summer.

What to do about them? In July, a gentle couple from the neighbourhood knocked on the front door collecting for an organization that wants to sterilize the deer, which, the couple told us, is a humane way to keep their numbers down. It's either that or they're going to the pound, I thought, something people say to encourage the adoption of abandoned cats and dogs.

For a crazed moment, I thought the couple wanted money to buy books on castration techniques to take care of the problem themselves, and pictured the scene – tranquilizer guns, dolly, hoists, knives, carport – and almost laughed in their earnest faces. Because, while outraged at the devastation deer are capable of, my level of outrage is not as high as some people's; I'm somewhat laissez-faire about them. And most of us are learning to adjust. Fencing, planting deer-proof plants, like lavender and herbs, not planting tulips, shooing them away.

Our son Bill and his wife Melanie watched this past spring as a doe gave birth to twins on the back lawn of their rented house in Victoria. They videoed the event, posted it on Facebook, and received many comments from their friends in response, most containing the word "awesome."

I have to agree. The deer are sleek, beautiful creatures. They are the closest most of us will ever come to viewing large wildlife at close range. Even while standing calmly in threes and fours on our back lawn, they seem otherworldly in their apartness, like phantoms sauntering through a dream.

27

AUDUBON SOCIETY

Dear Helen,

Since I've been focusing on the practice of gardening as a way to handle the "personal strain" of living through terrifying times, and as a way of not losing heart and of finding the hope to do this, articles and books about the benefits of gardening seem to have been flying at me. It lends truth to the comment made by American journalist Gene Weingarten, who said in an online interview about his book *One Day* that "The deeper you drill into anything, the more eerily intertwined things become."

What's in play here is the principle of "like-attracting-like," the noticing of things which are the same as your new experience. When you get pregnant, you see pregnant women everywhere. When you get a dog, everyone has the same breed (labs, doodles, pugs) at the end of the same blue retractable leash.

When our granddaughter was born, I started seeing newborns everywhere, but not in the way you'd expect. Shortly after her birth, I imagined people transformed into the newborns they once were. I watched them giving IVs in the hospital, filling out charts, delivering meal trays. Outside the hospital, I watched them driving cars, changing lanes; waiting in bank lineups; wearing backpacks along city streets; checking their phones. Terry and I at the dinner table were newborns too, clinking glasses with friends, also newborns. All of us red-faced and swaddled, still amazed by our grown-up lives, yet with our helpless beginnings on show. TV news anchors were especially vivid in this regard.

One article I read about gardening was from the Audubon Society urging gardeners not to be too tidy in their gardens this fall. "Messy gardens are good for birds and bugs," it said, urging us to leave seed heads from flowers for wintering birds and piles of leaves for smaller wildlife to hide in.

At this juncture, and in my own defence, since I am a committed raker of leaves, I'm applying the Audubon Society's advice to the "wild part" of our yard, the place where birds and bugs will surely find a home this winter once again. This is where I dump most of the leaves I rake. It's a rather unkempt area – a largish strip of land on the west side of the house. It includes an arbutus tree, two mid-size fir trees that were given to our kids in elementary school as seedlings, underbrush, ferns, salal, Terry's rough bike shed, and a winding pathway he hacked through several years ago. Also in residence, in hiding, are several spent Christmas trees, plastic outdoor chairs, and a rusted barbecue, which the rabbits like.

28

THE YARD

About our place, Helen:

We usually say "yard" when referring to the area around our house, seldom "garden." Calling it a garden when we moved in sounded pretentious, and we've largely avoided that reference. It was a fairly bare lot in a semi-rural area when we bought it, except for a few oak and maple trees along the roadside. The yard remained untended for several years, until the kids grew older, and we had enough energy to give it some attention.

We bought the southwest-facing half-acre in 1979 for a pittance by today's prices, and then built the house, which was designed by Terry's architect brother-in-law, Norman Dobell. All of us admired the work of Frank Lloyd Wright in those days (and still do) but the design Norman came up with – windows spanning the entire length of the two-level house, dramatic deck wings off either end – was too fabulous for the mortgage requirements, and we had to scale back the square footage. Originally, the house we had in mind was to be a modest cottage, but Norman would have none of that. "How will you ever have cocktail parties in such poky rooms?" he asked, advocating for the "open plan."

So, we went ahead, Terry and his builder-brother, Rickey, doing the work alongside friends of theirs, who were in the trades. I was thirty-two at the time with an eighteen-month-old baby who was recovering from whooping cough. Terry was five years older. We'd never built a house before. Sleep-deprived because of the baby, I could not imagine myself hosting a cocktail party, or even wearing a dress. But Norman altered the house design to meet the bank's requirements and we have always been glad of the open space. With the new, smaller design, we were able to keep the spanning windows on the top level and one of the decks. My father, who'd rented his entire life, said we were out of our minds to build a house. "Think of the upkeep," he told us. "Think of replacing the roof! What if the house burns down?"

The house was unfinished when we moved in, four months after the hole had been dug. It had bare floors, no cupboards or interior doors, no latches on the windows, and nothing but framing and sacks of pink insulation in the lower level.

I was soon pregnant again. So, there was no "upkeep," in my father's sense of the word, when it came to the yard. A large pile of dirt left from excavating for the foundation stayed for years where it was originally dumped. It became covered in mustard seed and toy trucks. "Go play on the dirt pile!" I'd holler at the kids, or at Terry when I was mad at him.

Somehow, we managed to plant two apple trees, a Mac and a Granny Smith, and a yellow plum tree, and then the seedlings people gave us for the kid's birthdays – a sequoia, a Norfolk pine. And then we found a blue spruce washed up on the beach, still in its Christmas-tree pot. We took it home and planted it by the mud room door. But mostly we just "stuck things in" – plants, shrubs, trees – without plan or vision. Some things lived, some didn't.

Scrolling through some notes yesterday, I came across a quote by Frank Lloyd Wright. It's waited eleven years to be used: "Study nature, love nature, stay close to nature. It will never fail you."

That dirt pile was "nature."

29

GERANIUMS

Dear Helen,

Remember when the irritating things we did were called "bad habits"? As a child, I was told that my bad habits included showing off, being too smart for my own good, having eyes in the back of my head, having my head in the clouds, being wound up tighter than a corkscrew, and chewing the ends of my hair. Sounds like a future writer to me.

Now, like many, I've acquired a new bad habit – the overuse of my phone. It's seduced me with the promise of instant fulfillment. All I have to do to achieve this state is to drop my criticisms, my questionings, my burrowing, annoying mind, and click "Like" or "Love" to everyone on the other side of the screen. And the clicking feels good, like I'm being a positive force in the world, a generous person. I can sprinkle faces with red hearts for eyes as the mood takes me, along with rainbows, bottles of champagne, white check marks in green squares, cartwheeling girls. I can approve your dinner, your dog, or your prize, and receive red and mauve hearts for my pictures of clouds. I can sign petitions to save the Amazon rainforest, grizzly bears, West Coast salmon, donate to GoFundMe sites, and feel part of some vague global solution.

I was thinking about the warmth of feeling the clicking world gives me when I noticed a hummingbird at the feeder on the back deck. Sitting in the sun with a cup of coffee at the time, my immediate thought was: "I'll grab a photo of that, post it, and then spend the rest of the day checking for 'likes' and 'loves,' and perhaps even flattering comments. This way I will feel loved and hopeful." Because, frankly, I was feeling low. It had to do with the absence of pollinating bees this year, and our barren yellow plum tree. It involved the pain in my left knee, and a generalized fear I was falling apart.

But I didn't take that picture. I stopped myself and asked, "What would Helen Chesnut do? Would she be checking her phone every hour to see if anyone liked her posts?"

No. She'd be focused on something important, like a Martha Washington geranium and how it needs a cool indoor temperature to survive the winter. She'd be advising A.H. on the correct way to plant a begonia cutting by using porous soil and a plastic bag for a tent.

I continued sitting in the sun and watched the hummingbird. I watched the breeze rustle the leaves of the tree that had no plums. I thought about pruning the zonal geraniums I'd recently moved inside. Like a holy rite, I've heard they love a hard pruning.

Then I read a few poems by the late James Tate, from his posthumous book, *The Government Lake*. One of the poems, "Roscoe's Farewell," is about an old dog that dies three times, and ends, "Roscoe disappeared forever among the flowerpots / and old tin cans, saying goodbye to this world, one last time."

After that, and despite the pain in my knee, I rode my bike two kilometres to the store to buy a lemon.

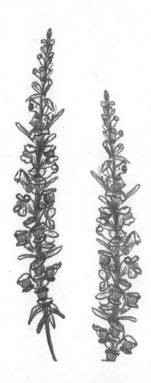

30

COMPOST

Dear Helen,

On a morning walk, we said hello to a woman we often see with her dogs. She stopped to tell us they had both "passed over" in recent weeks, and that this sad occurrence was the reason for their absence.

Later, I thought about the woman using the phrase "passed over." It reminded me of a column you wrote about getting rid of spent annuals. "Give them a decent rest on the compost pile," you said. And I thought: What a sensible statement to make about death! Kindness, acceptance, and purpose all in one sentence, so unlike the usual vague euphemisms we say when a death occurs.

I wondered where the woman's dogs had "passed over" to? But of course, I knew exactly what the woman meant: they had died, though "not really." Her dogs had moved to another dimension but were somehow still with her, and this belief gave her comfort. "Passing over" to the other side is the stuff of spirituals and the mythical boat ride captained by Charon.

The woman might have said her dogs had "gone to spirit," as a certain poet I know says with great reverence about the newly dead, but this expression, while similar to "passed over," didn't seem quite right for use by an elderly woman in rain gear.

But maybe not. Because I remembered she'd once told us that our dog, Lulu, was an "old soul." She said she could see it in the dog's eyes.

Being an "old soul," I later learned, means that some wise and benign spirit has reinhabited the world, in this case as Lulu, a malamute cross, though she has never been known as a gentle dog and was difficult to train. Still, hearing she was an "old soul" gave us a favourable way to view Lulu in the years ahead, gave us the tolerance we needed for her unpredictable ways, and I've always silently thanked the woman for her comment.

"The 'old soul' is off her game today," we'd say after she'd taken down a schnauzer, or nipped my ankle because I'd stepped on her tail.

Apparently, there are millions of "old souls" looking for homes but there are not enough homes to go around because there are more old souls out there than live bodies for them to inhabit. This was told to me some years ago by a Victoria hairdresser called Gerard of London, who seemed to be an authority on these things, and since then, I've been imagining bereft "old souls" fluttering about our heads like rapacious pigeons.

When Lulu died last spring we resorted to vagueness and told people she had "passed away." We might have said she had "evaporated," "disappeared," "departed forever," or simply, that she was "dead," but the expected expressions of distress on the faces of those we told forbade us to refer to her death in this way.

"She has 'passed away,'" we said, sadly, for we were sad. "We have her ashes in a silver urn and her paw print in plaster of Paris."

Many people sent sympathy cards, one, a bouquet of red tulips. The pet insurance company sent a cheque for $318 for the euthanasia and cremation costs. A picture of Lulu standing before a rainbow was posted on Facebook.

I like what you've so often suggested yourself, Helen, about gardens being metaphors for our lives: that our own growth cycles are like a garden, "moving inexorably from seedings to decline," or, as you've also said about spent annuals, moving to a happy home on the compost pile. I will keep this in mind when the time comes for my own "demise," and try to think of myself as a composted annual about to be of some use to the world. I'd like to achieve the same clear acceptance of life and death as you have before I start plucking the dead leaves from my hair in horror.

31

CLUBS AND MEETINGS

Dear Helen,

The gardening world is a vast and busy one. I know this because at the end of most of your columns you list local gardening events. Over the course of several columns, the list could run to pages. I'm coming to believe that these events are the places where a special kind of human decency lives.

There's the Chrysanthemum Meeting, the Lily Auction, the Orchid Meeting, and the Rose Meeting. There's a Floral Art Club, a Heather Society, a Dahlia Society, a Rhododendron Society, and a Native Plant Study Group presenting an evening slide show of subalpine wildflowers. The Vancouver Island Horticultural Society holds regular meetings and offers courses, some of them free. Local nurseries give classes on winter pruning and wreath-making. Each neighbourhood has a gardening club. There's the Family Harvest Festival, the annual Feast of the Fields, and, in our own area, the North Saanich Flavour Trail each August, which is billed as a two-day "celebratory rural ramble" by bike, car, or on foot to meet local growers, harvesters, vintners, and chefs.

The list is inspiring. To think that all these events and more are happening on the southern end of Vancouver Island, and that there are, without a doubt, similar events happening in every community across the country. To think that great numbers of positive and curious people are coming together to share their enthusiasm for growing things. Growing things! This, to some-one who puts a lot of effort into voicing her latest sardonic rant about living in a crazed world, is astounding news.

Beyond the pop-culture world and the book world, beyond the news world and the world of resistance movements, there's a large and dedicated community of benign, forthright people who are in love with their gardens, with nature, and with all living things. They give me hope for the future. They make me want to sing.

32

NAUGHTY MARIETTA

A flower story, Helen,

When I was nine or ten years old, I thought Elsie's declaration that she was going to plant Naughty Mariettas in the bed alongside the house was a reference to me, "Naughty Marion." That if I didn't smarten up, I'd be dug into the garden. It turns out she planted Naughty Mariettas *every* spring; I just hadn't noticed. It must have been my hearing the name for the first time that led me to pay attention.

The flowers, a yellow and maroon marigold, seemed to be her favourite. I didn't know why she loved them so much. I found them squat and boring, and she always planted them precisely, like a row of soldiers.

She seemed to like saying the name of the flower, as well. Combining "naughty" with a French or Italian name suggested a dangerously pert woman, something Elsie was not. Yet she changed her behaviour slightly when she said the words. Changed from being a short, plump woman wearing glasses into someone else, a vivacious Carmen with her hands on her hips, head thrown back, laughing.

The only time I ever saw Elsie wink lasciviously at Ernie was when she announced to him one Saturday morning that they needed to go to the nursery for some Naughty Mariettas. Ernie, who was usually much put upon by Elsie, and meek and cranky as a result, immediately perked up. He was at the breakfast table slathering jam on his toast and paused. Even though it was a Saturday, he was wearing the unglamorous clothes he wore to work as a janitor – beige pants and a matching shirt. But his manner when he heard the words, like Elsie's, changed; he sat up straight and cocked his head. "Oh yes," he said, and winked back at her. You'd think he was wearing a satin cape.

If I had known about planting seasons then, I would have suspected something was odd. It was November, not May, when those winks occurred.

As a young teenager, I'd often watch weekend late-night movies on TV with Elsie. She loved the musicals. We'd stay up past midnight, eating raisin toast and drinking weak tea. Ernie never watched the movies with us. He'd be snoring on the pullout in the basement if he'd been banished, or snoring in their bedroom, which was only a few feet away from the "den" where we were, if he hadn't. The den was the poky room facing the carport and had just enough space for a small colonial chesterfield and chair, two TV trays, and the black-and-white TV set.

One night, a movie starring Jeanette MacDonald and Nelson Eddy came on. The title was *Naughty Marietta*, and it was made in 1935. After the movie ended, I thought I understood why Elsie loved the flower. It was named after a movie that reminded her of falling in love.

Jeanette MacDonald plays a spunky princess who flees to France to escape an arranged marriage. Once there, she wears becoming milkmaid dresses and caps and sings her heart out. A handsome military man, Nelson Eddy, hears her lovely soprano and is soon singing with her.

Towards the end of the movie, when they declare their love and sing, "Ah! Sweet Mystery of Life," I glanced over at Elsie. She was crying.

Until then I had only thought of her as unaffectionate and bossy, as someone who never bent or cracked or had any fun. To see a different side of her gave me a jolt. There was more to Elsie than I'd ever imagined. She had a secret life! A tender heart!

Perhaps some kind of singing happened each time she and Ernie made up. Perhaps the words "Naughty Marietta" were code words for the happy ending to their rift. I can almost picture them singing a sweet duet in the car on the way to the nursery for the flowers.

But not really. "Don't crack me up!" she'd have said of my imaginings. She knew the truth of her dreams.

GARLIC

Dear Helen,

When eleven thousand scientists from around the world recently signed a letter saying the coming climate catastrophe is going to be worse than predicted, and listed the many ways it would be, making particular reference to the "untold human suffering" we should expect to occur, I fled to an old column of yours about growing garlic. Garlic, after all, reputedly wards off evil, and it would surely do its best with news like this.

To be fair, their mission was intended as a wake-up call for the rest of us to take climate change seriously, though I'm getting jumpy about receiving these incessant wake-up calls; they've become like random electric shocks. And I don't know many people now, besides a number of politicians, who are not taking things seriously, who are not nervously "awake."

The scientist's letter said they were "telling it like it is," and attempted, somewhat, to address the hopelessness of our situation.

"While things are bad, all is not hopeless," said lead author Dr. Thomas Newsome from the University of Sydney. "We can take steps to address the climate emergency." He cited children's activism, grassroots protests, reducing meat consumption and eating a plant-based diet, reducing tree cutting, reducing personal flying.

But eleven thousand scientists telling us that things are bad and going to get worse is the same as eleven thousand gods telling us the end is nigh. Weren't scientists supposed to replace gods in the hope department? Weren't they supposed to be working on a cure for *everything*?

What would eleven thousand Buddhas say? "A frog jumped into the water / Deep resonance" (Matsuo Bashō)?

What would my father, the sailor, say? "Steady as she goes"?

What did James Lovelock say? He's the maverick scientist from Cornwall, England, who developed the Gaia hypothesis that the Earth is a self-regulating superorganism. In a 2008 *Guardian* interview, he said, *cheerfully*, that the climate catastrophe is inevitable and that we should take the next twenty years to enjoy ourselves. So, if we can get our minds around it, in less than twenty years, "the excrement hits the air-conditioning fan," to use Vonnegut's lively phrase. Each year I do the math: How many years do we have left?

Lovelock's message? Prepare for the inevitable. Prepare for survival. Prepare for mass migrations, food shortages, energy shortages. Put our resources into these things; it will give people a sense of purpose. Learn how to grow our own food. Not growing food might otherwise mean not eating. Ultimately, he said, it's ourselves and our communities helping one another that will get us through.

We might add here Leonard Cohen's line from "The Future":

I've seen the nations rise and fall
I've heard their stories, heard them all
But love's the only engine
Of survival

Your recent column, Helen – "Food-Plant Guide Ideal Gift for Home Gardeners" – was both a book review and a quiet call by you to practise personal food sustainability. The book you reviewed, *Changing the Climate with the Seeds We Sow* by Dan Jason of Salt Spring Seeds, lists sixteen easy-to-grow nutritious foods, including potatoes and garlic.

·I grew up on stories of the Victory Gardens during World War II, and of a bread called the "Doris Grant loaf." The no-knead recipe was a simple one and quick to prepare. It used whole-wheat flour and yeast, but had only one rising, and took forty minutes to bake. The loaves could be produced between bombings, and thus the British population was saved from starvation.

This is an example of one person – a nutritionist, Doris Grant – making a difference.

Another person making a difference is a local woman in our present time. I read about her in the *Peninsula News Review*. A single mother of two boys, she's knitting hats – toques – for those struggling with poverty. She said she wanted to give back – to the food bank that helped her when she lost her job; to the various agencies that provided her family with clothing. First, she knit toques for the children who visited the food banks with their parents; then she knit toques for the parents themselves; and then she branched out by knitting toques for a homeless shelter.

When she ran out of wool and couldn't afford to buy more, she sent an email request for wool to a friend, who passed the email around, and before long the woman was getting messages from fifty people wanting to donate wool, wanting to knit for her.

34

PRACTICAL MAGIC

Dear Helen,

It's easy to grow garlic, you said in a recent column, adding that a clove planted in October will yield an entire bulb in July; plant many cloves and get many bulbs. The soil doesn't even have to be that good, you said, and you can grow garlic on a deck in pots, or in a small area of your garden. And you're right about garlic's no-fail quality. It's the only crop we've ever reliably grown, year after year.

I was twenty-two years old before I knew that garlic even existed. Growing up, food was plain: either mashed or fried. Greens were frozen peas or Brussels sprouts. Dessert was canned peaches and vanilla ice cream, sometimes brownies, the virgin kind. The only condiments in use were salt and pepper, and maybe a sprig of parsley if the cook wanted to splash out and get fancy.

It took a big, blonde hippie from California, who was visiting a friend of a friend, to herald a new culinary era for me. She arrived in her blue VW Beetle at the shared house where I was living, and proceeded to make salad dressing for the group's first meal together. I stress the words "make salad dressing," because, until then, salad dressing was either Thousand Island or French from a Kraft bottle. What Pamela did was take several cloves of garlic that she'd brought from California, smash them with the end of a carving knife, and add them to a mixture of olive oil, red-wine vinegar, dry mustard, honey, and salt and pepper. Shortly after, everyone lost their minds.

That era wasn't only about sex, drugs, and loud music. It was also about a revolution in the way we ate, about the discovery of garlic, brown rice, whole wheat, herb teas, pinto beans, and yogurt: in short, the practice of whole-foods eating. It's comforting to track a positive change like this. Eating a plant-based diet, as we're being advised to do in the coming years, shouldn't be that difficult a task.

The older generation hated the new food we were eating then, and this was extremely satisfying to us. They rebelled about it in their own way, too. My father, for example, announced that he never ate things beginning with the letter *y*, so don't give him yogurt. Ernie told me with disgust that "brown rice gets stuck in your turds and tears up your insides."

As for the ability of garlic to ward off bad vibes, I can't give the practice a good report. A few years ago, we strung garlands of it above the outside doors in the hope that our overstaying guests would take the hint and leave. It didn't work. The guests, distant relatives from Colorado, stayed on – and on. Only after the stated three weeks of their visit had elapsed did they pack their bags to leave. By then, we were barely speaking to each other. It was champagne at 10 a.m. on the July morning after they left.

I can, therefore, attest to the benefits of champagne.

35

EXISTENTIAL WEEDS

Dear Helen,

Have you ever written a column about weeds? If you have, I'd love to read it. Weeds are an integral part of the home gardener's life, aren't they? Because they're always budging in, wanting their way, spoiling the look of things. They're always having to be gotten rid of because of the nasty work they do robbing favoured plants of light and nutrients. There's even a gardening task called "weeding."

I often hear about weeds from my friends, the ones who are serious gardeners. Besides the deer, rabbits, and rats eating what they grow, weeds are the source of a never-ending assault on their lives. No one I know will use herbicides to get rid of them, so they pull them out by hand, or use black plastic sheeting with carefully cut-out holes to guard their tender lettuce and bean plants. They also use mulch, sawdust, and hay. Weeds command much of their time.

But there's another angle to weeds that I hadn't thought about – weed advocacy. In the book *Weeds: Guardians of the*

Soil by Joseph Coannouer, the author calls weeds "garden volunteers," and writes about the practice of permaculture, which is partially about putting weeds to work in the garden. Meaning, you no longer need to exclusively eradicate them, you can manage them. They have practical uses. Some, like dandelions and purslane, are edible; many provide ground cover or attract useful insects, such as ladybugs. And if you know what you're doing, some are medicinal.

Pulling out weeds has always been a satisfying chore for me, like raking, vacuuming, and tidying up, which are all the same thing, I suppose: a need for order, and a form of meditation. But I didn't consider that weeds could be useful. And I'd certainly never thought of each one of them as a tiny representative of the cosmos. But this was pointed out to me by a friend at a party.

Well along in the evening, after the wine, when the music had been turned down, and the tea was being served, she silenced the room with her quiet comment about the existential existence of a single weed.

I'm not sure what caused her to mention weeds at this time of night. Maybe we'd arrived at the moment when everyone starts thinking about death and the bigger picture, something I've noticed often happens at the end of a party. But Jane said, "That threadlike stem with its two tiny leaves, with its drive to live, is as astonishing to me as looking up at the galaxy of stars."

36

OLD SEEDS

Dear Helen,

"Boomers are not a dying breed." I read this in the morning paper. "Every eight minutes another boomer reaches sixty-five."

Like a plague of wizened rats cresting a hill, we keep on coming. There doesn't seem to be an end to us. This is the attitude of later generations, even though boomer births cover only the twenty years of post-WWII prosperity, 1945–1964.

I was born in the first wave, a couple of years after the war. Saying this has become like standing up at a meeting and saying you're an alcoholic. Except there is no twelve-step program I can join to make amends for the fact that my generation got everything – educations, jobs, houses, general practitioners, fresh air, toys, trips, leisure, and often peace.

The article about boomers was in the Business section. It highlighted the continued importance of boomers because they bought 41 percent of the snacks, and 46 percent of the candy in the fifty-two weeks ending in April of last year. "They are single-handedly keeping the economy afloat," the article said.

Here's a mental image of a boomer sitting in an armchair, rereading *One Flew Over the Cuckoo's Nest* by Ken Kesey while listening to the Stones' "Sympathy for the Devil" and eating sour-cream and green-onion potato chips. What a time I'm having keeping the economy afloat!

Ooo, who, who. Ooo, who, who.

On that note, I once danced with Ken Kesey at a "Symposium on Freedom," which was organized by the University of Victoria on Vancouver Island at an inn. The dancing was nothing, a random thing on a crowded dance floor. I was twenty-three years old at the time and Kesey would have been around thirty-five. He was a short, muscular man wearing a white shirt, jeans, and cowboy boots with heels, and had bits of fluffy hair here and there on his balding head. He and the Merry Pranksters had arrived at the symposium out of nowhere. It was more of a be-in than a symposium.

At some point during the day, everyone had a look at the Prankster's famous psychedelic bus parked in the driveway. I remember feeling nothing much about it, no matter how hard I tried. The symposium was held on a Saturday, the same day, it turned out, that Richard Nixon announced he was resigning as president of the United States.

I think we can agree that the boomer generation has, above all else, been a searching and freewheeling one. Some of its members are still like that. My friend, Gerald, from high school, for example. Here's an illustration of enlightenment he made not long ago, after years of weed-guided study. It seems to represent a particular experience of the genus *Existentialis weedii*, one that moves beyond astonishment.

"I finally got it right," he said when he showed the illustration to me.

I promised I would pass it around. Here it is.

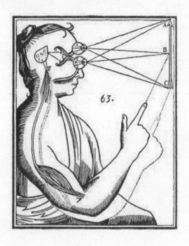

It has a certain *something*, don't you think?

37

OPERETTA

Act 1

Your headline in this morning's column, Helen – "Hastily Planted Flower Patch Gives Glorious Display of Colour" – spoke about a last-minute planting you did that turned out well. The flowers were purple cosmos, a plant, you said, that was "well loved for its large daisy-type flowers on tall, feathery bushes." You also praised late marigolds, the blooms of which "add light citrus notes to salads."

A pleasing thought. Light notes in the salad, like the chorus in an operetta.

Act 2

That evening, at a birthday party, a woman told me that the thing that marks a gardener as a beginner is that they plant mostly pink flowers. It was a wasp-sting comment, but she couldn't have known about my neophyte gardening status, that my theme last year was pink – petunias, geraniums, and impatiens.

The woman, whose name was Dorothy, was a veteran gardener and also an artist, who had trained in design and now
worked as the head props person at an opera company. She said
she devoted half her life to her garden, and that besides growing
apples, blueberries, and raspberries, she planted flowers, but only
red, orange, and yellow ones. This was because her house, she
said, was painted blue, red, orange, and yellow, and the flowers
matched. I asked if there was grass, and she said, "Just a little,
as an accent."

I wondered what her garden would look like and made a
mental note to drive by. Then I wondered what three-colour
combination I would choose for my garden this spring. Not
pink, not anymore, though I like pink. But I also like white
flowers, so that's useful. Over the winter, I could start solving
the puzzle of choosing. It would be an absorbing task and give
me something to think about other than, *Should I buy survival
backpacks for the kids to carry in the trunks of their cars?* This
has been on my mind a lot.

Act 3

Hours later, I had a private gardening consultation with Dorothy.
This happened in a dream. She appeared as a clairvoyant offering
advice from inside a tent. Her appearance was the same as at
the party, a small, sixtyish woman in brown pants and flowered
top, except that instead of short spikey hair, she had long braids
affixed at the end with pink plastic bows, her only eccentricity.
The consultation cost twenty dollars.

"Why are you here?" she asked.

"I want my garden to be filled with tall feathery bushes," I said.

"In time perhaps, not now," she said.

"Why not?"

"Because you are a beginner. Plant light notes in the garden. Flowers that are pink. They're the mark of a beginner gardener. Why not celebrate what you are?"

"But I want this year's colours to be blue and white," I said. "Surely, blue and white is the mark of a sophomore. Can't I be a sophomore? I want forget-me-nots and white cosmos. The theme will be mortal existence."

"The theme is always mortal existence," she said. "But, dear, after four decades, you are still a beginner gardener. You will never become a master, there isn't enough time. And mastery isn't the point of a beginner's garden. The point is accomplishment. Never is it glory."

"Yes, yes," I said.

"Isn't it pleasant being a beginner?" she asked. "No one expects much of you, and if you do achieve something of note, everyone cheers."

"Do marigolds count? I want banks of marigolds for my summer salads."

"Ah, marigolds," she said. "I don't praise them. Their blooms hang on too long. They're like opera singers performing way past anyone's interest."

"What else can you tell me?"

"Buy survival packs for your children. Doing so will help you sleep at night."

"Anything else?"

"Yes. Use grass sparingly."

38

ROOKIE

Dear Helen,

For some strange reason there was a different gardening column planted above yours in the Sunday paper this morning. It was by Dean Fosdick, and the paper said it was brought to us from the Associated Press news service. Dean Fosdick must have listened in on my dream about Dorothy the other night because he wrote, "There is such a thing as being too enthusiastic, especially among novices." His column was about the mistakes rookie gardeners routinely make, and included: thinking too big, planting in the wrong location, having an unreliable water source, planting in poor soil, not keeping gardening records, not dealing quickly with insects or weeds, and overcrowding.

I am guilty on all counts. The list sums up everything I have ever done wrong in the garden, and I ask myself, "If you were really passionate about gardening, don't you think you would have corrected these mistakes before now?"

It's beginning to dawn on me that there's such a thing as being *unenthusiastic* about gardening. I loathe to admit it, but my interest has always been sporadic and half-hearted. I'm as lackadaisical about gardening as I have ever been about anything.

It's the word "job" that stops me. Here's a definition I found online from the *Cambridge Dictionary* that confirms my feeling: it says the word "gardening" means, "the job or activity of working in a garden, growing and taking care of the plants, and keeping it attractive." What this really means is that gardening is often back-breaking, sweat-producing, *hard physical work*, something I have never – how can I put this? – been overly fond of. I'll sedately pick flowers or gaze in appreciation at someone else's garden, but I will never be heard giving this heated cry: "Give me that pickaxe [or crowbar or backhoe]! I'll get the damn job done!"

Other than the pleasure I experienced planting daffodil bulbs in the fall, and noticing this week that sixty-one of the eighty bulbs are showing shoots, I haven't, to date, been gripped by a passion for growing things. Like Alice, it seems I'm either too small or too big to fit through this particular doorway to bliss.

But I'm trying not to be discouraged. I'm hoping that if I persevere, a love of gardening (if not hard labour) will *in some form* overtake me. Thinking about the need now, and in the near future, for family food gardens; admiring flower gardens; reading your columns; enjoying Brett's fresh vegetables; reading the exuberant Elizabeth von Arnim. These things might help me achieve a sustained interest. Von Arnim writes, in *Elizabeth and Her German Garden*, of "keen air bracing the soul" each time she enters her garden. Even though she had years of trials and disappointments over its creation, she still maintained a heady love for it. "Keen air" and a "bracing soul" are wonderful things to experience, but, for me, these things mostly occur on my daily walks.

Would the love of gardening give me the same delight I get while viewing clouds, I wonder? Or the same thrill I'm experiencing with the online course about crows that Terry gave me? (Did you know, Helen, that the much-maligned crow is not the greatest eater of baby birds in their nests? Squirrels and snakes are the main culprits, followed by racoons.)

But lusting after any kind of love doesn't work, as we all know. You will never get your heart's desire by grasping after it. What you will get are people being embarrassed on your behalf and looking at the ceiling when you enter a room.

The realization I'm coming to is that I am not alone, that there are other people in the world, who, like me, have this defect, this lack of gardening passion. This was confirmed when I overheard an elderly woman in the Beacon Café last week talking with her three friends over coffee.

She said: "Fred wanted a garden but he never went out in it. It was the front garden he liked, not the back. The back was just grass and two plum trees. He couldn't care less about that. So, it was the garden that faced the street he obsessed about. Every winter he'd read the seed catalogues and tell me what to order. I'd get gardening gloves for Christmas without fail, or books about growing zinnias or perennials. Once, he gave me a gift-wrapped trowel. In spring, he'd stand on the porch and supervise me doing the planting. He'd remind me to water, or deadhead, or cut the grass. When everything was in bloom, he'd sit on the porch and look at it. People walking by would compliment him on his beautiful garden. He'd smile and say, 'Thank you.' When he died, I paved it over. The whole front yard – the beds, the grass, everything. It wasn't revenge, but really."

Two of the women laughed uproariously, but the third pursed her lips and looked away.

39

THREE BLACK DAISIES

Dear Helen,

My friend Lynn has recently given me a foldable vase. You fill the vase with water and it stands up. It's reusable, made of soft, green plastic, and is eight inches tall. When compressed, it's the size of a small wallet.

Lynn says I can take it with me when I go on holiday. Then I can buy cut flowers and, instead of using the drinking glass from the hotel bathroom as a vase, I can use the foldable one to make my room look pretty. It was a considerate gift from a person who travels often. She loves the vase and thought I would too.

Green leaves and black stems decorate the vase and the package provides instructions for its use. They're numbered one to four, and are printed on the back, which also shows a tap with water filling the vase, and another image of three black daisies standing erect with their stems crossed. It's made in China and costs $2.69 plus tax. You can buy one at the Dollar Store.

The actual name of the vase is Easy Vase. A green arrow at the bottom of the package points towards the small print, which says the owner of the vase can scan the barcode with their smartphone to learn more. I want to learn more. I always want to learn more, but I doubt if Easy Vase can teach me more than what is offered on the package.

I want to know, for example, about the steps that went into the manufacture and distribution of this plastic vase. I want to know who the person is who dreamed it up and why. Did they patent the vase? Have they made any money from it? Or were they team members, poorly paid factory employees, whose job it is to come up with products for the rapacious Western market? What are their thoughts about the plastic-clogged state of our oceans? And what about their families? How are they all getting on?

The vase was a gift, and is not to be maligned, even while presenting me with an ethical dilemma over its use. Now, because of this gift, I can make flower arrangements instantly, any-where, any time.

I think the plastic vase also qualifies as a spiritual gift because the flower, grass, and twig arrangements I can make while I'm away are designed to be temporary, as in, impermanent, though the plastic vase itself is not. Another use for it would be to facil-itate a sudden desire for beauty.

Speaking of impermanence, I recently saw a Buddha candle for sale that was made of beeswax. It was nine inches tall, cost forty-five dollars, and was featured at a store that sells honey. The idea behind the candle, I suppose, is that you can watch as the Buddha melts away, and that this slow melting will give you an illustration of impermanence in action, so to speak. Thus, you will become enlightened, though unsettling things about your life might be revealed as well.

I liked the idea of filling the Easy Vase with something – happiness, perhaps, because it is also impermanent, or rocks, because they're often not – and giving it to someone at the Vancouver bus stop where I was recently waiting in the rain for the #5 bus. This is what Mr. Bean would do, and it would be charming. He'd be wearing a bow tie and a sports jacket, and would pop out from behind the Plexiglas bus shelter and present three black daisies in the plastic vase to seventeen tired commuters. All-round delight would ensue, as the fierce young people I'd been watching would soften and laugh, become children again, and the other waiting bus passengers would start dancing. An impromptu musical number would happen next, with more dancers emerging from stopped cars, and it would become a wonderful, uplifting sight that would be videoed and shared worldwide.

Mr. Bean has that effect on people. Mr. Bean for President.

But of course, if I were to pop out from nowhere and present a bouquet of anything at a bus stop, I'd cause alarm. I understand this. People would become afraid of me; a police car might appear. Because I'm too old for spontaneous public acts of joy, which is too bad, but there I am an ordinary-looking woman who wears knee-length coats, and clogs, and sometimes glasses, and getting long in the tooth.

I had been in Vancouver for a literary reading, a dismal affair involving five other readers, seating for two hundred, and an audience of twelve.

When the bus arrived after the reading, the downpour had become sideways rain because of the wind. My ego must have come off that night because I awoke the next morning to find it at the foot of my bed at the Barclay Hotel. It was the size of a shroud made of see-through plastic. It was yellowed, cracked in places, and bent in an awkward foetal position, as if in pain.

To think that for all these years I'd been wearing it unsuspecting. That it had been getting in the way of direct experience, distorting all that I thought and felt.

I left it at the hotel for the cleaners to get rid of. I had the plastic vase in my purse, and that morning in room 212, I filled it with my shredded ego. I'm glad it's gone.

Actually, I'm trembling.

40

SLUG DEATH

Here's another gardening dream, Helen. It's about the lethal insecticide Corry's Slug & Snail Death, commonly called "Slug Death," a product from the middle of the last century that was meant to stop slugs and snails from eating infant vegetable plants. You might remember it. I'm not sure if it's still on the market because it killed a lot of other things besides slugs and snails – birds, racoons, pets – and people became alarmed and stopped using it.

In the dream, I'd found an "heirloom" package of Slug Death in the tank of our toilet. It was secured inside a taped metal box. I thought Terry had hidden it as my Christmas present and became excited. This feeling quickly changed to one of shame when I discovered what was in the tin and realized I'd hidden the box there myself.

Why would I do such a thing, since I have never used Slug Death and have banned all poison from our yard for decades? But it soon became obvious to me that the dream wasn't interested in my virtuousness, or my outrage at being falsely accused, or my terror of harming a child, or a pet, or anyone else with a lethal product.

The dream was about revisiting childhood. Slug Death was the portal.

Because there was my uncle Ernie kneeling at the side of our house at Cordova Bay during a windstorm. He was holding a box of Slug Death in his gloved hand, and sprinkling the contents, a white powder, like crematorium ash, around the row of marigolds, and then among a bed of purple petunias. The powder was flying about because of the wind, and Ernie was hollering at me to stay back – "For God's sake, don't you have any sense?"

This happened during the era which has since become famous for having a special kind of dumbness. It was the time of career housewives and John Cheever husbands, that is to say, of angry, overworked "heavy drinkers," who travelled long distances to their jobs as salesmen, executives, tradesmen. It was also the time of painting with lead, smoking a cigarette after sex, having "one for the road" before leaving a party, and using lethal chemicals around the house as a matter of course. I'm thinking of the Raid we sprayed on wood bugs in the bedrooms and flies in the kitchen. Actually, Elsie used it everywhere, like air freshener. Oddly, this has become a fond memory of home.

As a roaming girl, I loved the smell of skunk cabbage in the spring. It had a sharp, sweet odour similar to that of Raid. The skunk cabbages grew in the shaded creeks of the forests where my friends and I played, and they were exotic compared with the usual scrub of salal bushes and English ivy, and the fir and cedar trees that were about. One or two feet tall at maturity, the cabbages had bright yellow inside leaves and embracing outer leaves that were dark green and waxy. They were like nothing else in the forest.

There were often fat banana slugs on the sloping banks near the skunk cabbages, which, for some reason gave me a tender feeling when I saw them, perhaps because, blob-like and without bones, they looked so vulnerable, like exposed internal organs. About five inches in length, the slugs were a dull yellow in colour with black blotches over their backs. They had two swivelling tentacles, and travelled on their own excreted slime, which was a fascinating thing to know. My affection for banana slugs was confirmed years later after reading the prose poem "With Sincerest Regrets" by the American poet Russel Edson. The poem begins, "Like a monstrous snail a toilet slides into a living room on a track of wet, demanding to be loved."

In the present era, which has its own deadly dumbness, there are still frightening stories about the use of slug poison. I can barely mention the one about a nineteen-year-old Australian boy who, in 2010, ate a slug on a dare. The slug was infested with rat lungworm, and the boy became an instant paraplegic, dying eight years later.

Add eating slugs to all the other stupid things nineteen-year-old boys will do. The list includes diving into empty swimming pools, climbing cable towers while blind drunk, driving cars while semi-conscious, hurling themselves off cliffs into lakes and breaking necks and backs, poking eyes out while horsing around, and taking LSD alone in a forest at night and drowning in a puddle. This happened to the brother of a high-school friend.

Keeping my kids alive during their teenage years was the hardest work I have ever done.

About the small garden slugs that terrorize home gardens, I've learned there are safe and natural ways to eliminate them. But as with all such remedies, time and effort are required. You can, as a practice of mindfulness, pick them off at dawn or dusk and drop them into a pail of water, where they drown. You do this calmly, one slug at a time, during your out-breath. Or, you can put saucers filled with beer in various places around the garden, because slugs are fond of beer. During the night, they will congregate at the saucers and drink and drink. It's like they're hanging out at a notorious mollusc tavern. Death by alcohol poisoning soon follows.

41

NOURISHMENT

Dear Helen,

When I read that the Rolling Stones were going on a new world tour – no wait, maybe not, because Mick is recovering from open-heart surgery and Keith has fallen out of a tree – I wondered if this is something I should care about, and, if so, why?

Helen, do you know what I'm talking about? I think you might because in a recent column about "maturing" gardens you quoted Keith Richards: "I'm not ageing. I'm evolving."

My questions are these: Is the news of the Stones' upcoming world tour about the endurance of a hardy perennial rock band? An illustration of "abracadabra," of giving your fire until the end of your days? A homily about old folks still getting it on, shaking their booty? A bid for ticket sales? A claim for having our souls continually touched through music? Or is the information another example of a mindless pull into distraction?

Lately, when I read or listen to news that I can do nothing about other than weep or rage, I distract myself with something more immediate. The world of fallen leaves is my usual recourse.

I thank you and your columns for helping me do this. And my own reviving good sense about maintaining calmness in the face of calamity.

Here's an example. Yesterday was bright and warm, one of those rare November days without rain. I'd had a cold last week and stayed inside, the result being that masses of sweetgum and weeping willow leaves covered the driveway and half of the back lawn.

I couldn't wait to get at them, and did so in the afternoon, with our other cat, Ray, a ginger, as my companion. He's eighteen months old, with shiny orange and white fur, and is bursting with good health. What better way to spend an afternoon than outside in the sunshine with a simple task to complete, with Ray tearing up the willow tree, then jumping onto the raked leaves beneath it, then throwing himself at my feet to be petted and loved?

There was a time when Terry might have done these things out of the sheer joy of my presence, but just then he was inside following the news of the cabinet shuffle on his phone.

"No blame," as the sages say.

"It furthers one to cross the great water," they also say.

Which I did by singing the refrain from "Gimme Shelter" into Ray's rapt yellow eyes.

42

SOIL

Dear Helen,

Preserving garden soil over winter is the topic of your column today. It focuses on the distinction between ornamental gardens (flowers, shrubs, grasses) and vegetable gardens (food). Both garden types need their soils protected over winter; both have their own requirements.

Straightforward comments like this are a revelation to me. You make such distinctions often and they are as tidy, I'm certain, as your garden beds are. My gardening distinctions have always been muddy – flowers, vegetables, dirt – it's all one thing. Roses no different than grass. Their needs – sunshine and water – the same. I know. I know.

But a garden or a life is not a philosophical theory or an idea or a system of thought. It's a tangible thing, situated in the phenomenal world, and perceptible through immediate experience. This seems obvious now.

Garden soil, you write, "is a life-giving community of organisms and micro-organisms that are a source of health for the plants we grow."

So are human communities, and I'm drawn to the words "protection" and "life-giving" in the column with regard to this. There are not many instances of an individual thriving alone.

43

STAKES

Dear Helen,

A column of yours last fall about pruning roses mentioned the climbing variety and the importance of having a secure support as an aid for their upward growth – a trellis, netting, or stakes.

As we know, a child needs the same kinds of supports. They need to be held up – guided – as they grow and, if they are fortunate, this is done by a person or people who have a "stake" in their outcome, that is, who love them and want the best for them. This "staking" is done, in part, by tending to the child's early growth, ensuring ongoing basic care, and by praising their "blooms," their milestones, as they arrive, year after year.

Though he was often relegated by Elsie to the sidelines, Ernie was one of my supports growing up, albeit an unassuming one. Short, pudgy, bespeckled, and bald, he may have engaged in an ongoing battle with his wife, and was cranky at times as a result, but he was a kindly man at heart. I spent a lot of time with him. The things he did for me were many: teaching me how to ride a bike, train my dogs, drive a car; keeping me company after school watching TV cartoons; picking me and my teenage friends up from Friday Night Skate in Victoria; driving me wherever I wanted to go since we lived in an area without public transport. When I was sixteen, he got me my first job waitressing at Evelyn's Cafe next to the Victoria Public Library. Most importantly, he often took my side in arguments with Elsie. I loved him quietly, steadfastly, in a child's secure way, knowing he would remain one of the "stakes" holding up my world.

He was the quiet half of the duo when I came to live with him and Elsie when I was five. They'd married seven years earlier, when they were both in their forties. Elsie frequently told me I was the child they couldn't have, which was a confusing thing to know with having an absent mother in Australia and a father in Vancouver. Suddenly there were four parents, each with a unique role; I was often unsure where my allegiance should lie.

I was twenty-three years old, newly working at the children's treatment centre up the road, when Ernie died. And how ironic that his death happened on Elsie's sixty-fifth birthday, March 31. It was as if by dying on that date he was giving her an inappropriate birthday gift, while at the same time having the last word in one of their fights. Instead of slamming the front door and retreating to his outside workshop, as he usually did in the heat of battle, he died – dramatically.

I'd stopped by the Cordova Bay house that morning with Elsie's present, which was three yards of pink cotton boucle because she liked to sew, and after all those birthdays I'd run out of ideas. I thought the present would be something different and was excited to give it to her. I pictured her making a summer pants-and-top outfit, like the one she'd made herself in yellow.

I parked my car and walked in the front door. Elsie and my father, Billy, were sitting in what Elsie called the den, a tiny room at the front of the house looking onto the driveway. The TV set was in there but was turned off. Elsie was on the colonial chesterfield doing nothing; Billy was on the blue recliner with his sock feet tucked beneath him. He was drinking from a bottle of rye. It was on the TV tray beside him. This was the first shock – that he was drinking at ten in the morning – that he was drinking at all. He held a glass of straight rye in his hand.

Elsie said, "Ernie's dead. It just happened. They took him away. He got out of bed and dropped dead. They said he was dead before he hit the ground."

It would have happened in the room he shared with Billy, my former bedroom. They had twin beds in there now. Elsie had the double in the other bedroom. This arrangement had gone on for three or four years, since Billy moved in when he retired.

Billy had on a navy-blue polo shirt that morning. For some reason I noticed that. And his face, which was flushed all the way to his forehead. Elsie was still in her pink dressing gown.

She said, "I'd just taken him some hot lemon. He said he wasn't feeling good. I thought he was getting a cold. But he looked grey. I said, 'I'd better take you to the hospital.' He started to get up. I was standing right there. He pulled the covers away – his legs were bare – and he stood up. Then he fell. I tried to move him off the floor, but he was too heavy. I called Billy. We both tried to move him, but we couldn't. You could tell he was dead. Billy called the ambulance. I put a blanket over his legs."

44

NAVIGATION

Dear Helen,

Turning to your columns for metaphors and practical advice has become something of an anchor for me. They are not only about the art and skill of gardening but can be read as being about the art and skill of living, as well. What are Buddhism or Taoism or the *I Ching* or even a twelve-step program about, if not a series of travel tips for navigating a journey through life with the least amount of suffering? In this regard, advice about tending a garden is a kind of travel tip.

We constantly look to each other for guidance and explanation. For directions about how to live well. For homilies to aid us in handling the storms that spin us out of orbit, the unexpected calamitous events that render us lost, without bearings.

When the time came, I looked to my father and my aunt for the best way to raise our children. I naturally discounted my mother's lack of involvement as a model. It was predictable love and wholesale support from my father, and routine, basic care and loyalty to family from Elsie that I followed. Their way of raising me, along with my own creative bent, are what I believed saved me from a childhood of chaos and the subsequent fall-out. In my early twenties, I worked at Sevenoaks, a residential treatment centre for "emotionally disturbed children," and it was there that I came to understand the trajectory of my own childhood – that I was not disturbed myself, as I had feared. I'd simply been lucky to be raised as I was.

As an adult, I've collected quotes and sayings to help me navigate through the days and years – many people do – the quotes changing over time. They provide sightlines, direction posts, and I catch them from everywhere, magpie fashion. From something read, or something heard. From philosophers, writers of fiction, memoir, and poetry; from essays about the natural world and articles about healthy eating; from songs and movies; from your gardening columns.

My progress towards understanding myself and my world has had its ups and downs, though; life is messy, emotions often rule, and I can get sidetracked and fall down holes of worry and doubt. Nevertheless, I keep at it because I see the results – an aerating of the mind, a freeing from trellising biases.

Here are two quotes I particularly like. They're from Kurt Vonnegut's *A Man without a Country*, his last book, and, perhaps, his last word on the subject of "navigation." The first concerns what it was, besides music, that made his life "almost worth-while": "All the saints I met ... people who behaved decently in a strikingly indecent society." The second: "There's only one rule that I know of, babies – God damn it, you've got to be kind."

45

DAWN

Dear Helen,

For a few days this winter I looked out the bedroom windows in the early morning instead of looking at the news on my phone the moment I woke up. This outward looking, I decided, would be about paying attention to the rising day instead of to the timeless global news cycle. It seemed a sensible thing to do and would be a kind of meditation while still in bed, sitting up with the quilt around my shoulders.

There are three large windows in the room. Most of the time I would stare at the blackness outside because, at this time of the year, sunrise doesn't happen until 8 a.m. But I soon found that the blackness was boring, that I had nothing to think about it, and nothing to see in it, not even a street light. I would sit staring for a long, cold time into nothing before a lightening of the sky occurred, and the first tree outlines appeared – willows, poplars, oaks, firs. I did this for four mornings. Two mornings were clear – a thin line of peach light becoming visible in the east – and then two more mornings were uninterestingly grey.

I abandoned the practice because of the cold, and because the cats took my sitting up as the signal I was about to feed them and started tearing about. But I'd made the point to myself: It was possible to avoid the early morning distress caused by my news addiction, and, in doing so, I could set myself up for a lighter-feeling day.

During this self-imposed regime, my evening reading was Elizabeth von Arnim's *The Solitary Summer*. It's about the months she spent on her German estate in the 1920s, "alone" with her children and servants, but mostly by herself in her garden, the place, she says, that had overtaken her "body and soul." Many of von Arnim's books are about the particulars of this all-encompassing love and were written during a time when women of her class didn't get their hands dirty. Because of this social constriction, she had to hire labourers, often ineffectual, and longed to do the heavy work herself. In this she prevailed, her gardening passion being very much a creative rebellion against her husband (the "Man of Wrath"), her gender, and her class. Fortunately, she had the wealth and strength of character to pretty much do as she liked.

Dawn, she wrote, can be a frightening time if there is no one else about, not even an animal; it is still and quiet and you are seeing things as they are – before human intervention or commentary skews the vision. Von Arnim's vision of dawn happened when she wandered out at 4 a.m. on a June morning. She said, "I was frightened by the awful purity of nature, when all the sin and ugliness is shut up and asleep, and there is nothing but beauty." When full daylight arrived, she called it "the unbearable, indifferent brightness."

I've experienced the strangeness of a summer morning when I've woken early and gone for a walk. There's a feeling of trespass then, even voyeurism, and there's an eerie stillness. You are walking about in a world in which human consciousness is mostly absent. Other things – houses, cars, trees, stop signs – exist profoundly in their own right, cold and brutal in their apartness.

It's the same intrusive feeling I get walking into someone's home when they aren't there. The sofa, the framed family pictures on the sideboard, the kettle on the stove, the dog dish beside the broom. It's too intimate. I'm embarrassed to have seen it naked, avert my eyes, hurry away.

46

PURPOSE

Dear Helen,

Your column today gave me a sense of your environmental concerns. The headline was, "Home Garden Is Your Own Little Recycling Depot," and you began the column with a not-quite-enraged comment about the amount of food the average household wastes in a week – five and a half pounds – and what we can do about that.

What followed were tips for recycling this waste into the garden – food scraps into the compost, newspaper and cardboard to line a pathway before the straw goes on. You called the practice "great opportunities for good" and also mentioned buying wax-coated food wrappers for use instead of single-use plastic.

About living a purposeful life: I happened across an article about the residents of the California town of Loma Linda, who, because of the way they live – vegan, vegetarian, or little meat, daily exercise, service to the community, scant alcohol, no smoking – live, on average, eight to ten years longer than anyone else in the U.S. Most of the residents are members of the Seventh-day Adventist Church.

"I never had stress," said a one-hundred-year-old resident, who was still cutting his own lawn. "I have a philosophy: You do the best you can. And the things you can't do anything about, don't give any thought to them."

Doing the best you can. It's a thought simple enough to faith a life.

Another perspective comes from someone who is also doing the best she can – a thirty-seven-year-old friend of my daughter, who is a single mother of ten-year-old twin girls. She's aware of the threatening state of things, she says, but hates the word "activist" because being an activist about the climate apocalypse is not something she can manage right now.

"After a full day's work, it's all I can do to drive home, pick up the kids from after-school care, and cook supper," she says. "Keeping my kids healthy and my home together is activism enough."

Writer and botanist Diana Beresford-Kroeger, in her book *The Sweetness of a Simple Life*, urges each of us worldwide to embrace the practice of planting a tree. Doing so would be a vital help to the atmosphere, and give us purpose, she writes. "Together we can hold hands across the planet and repair the damage done in the past five hundred years," she says. "We will make a difference to nature, one by one and tree by tree."

47

OUT THERE

Dear Helen,

These days, I approach your columns with humility. I've learned to accept that I'm a beginner gardener, and most likely always will be.

I mentioned before about gardening not being something I've naturally loved. I could tell you where my love for any number of other things comes from, but gardening? There is nothing there. I have no tender gardening memories. Where does this love of not-gardening come from?

My family. They had little regard for the natural world – but few people in the middle of the twentieth century did. My family called anything that wasn't a house, a store, or a building "out there." And aside from sunsets and days at the beach, "out there" was a boring place, only useful for driving through. And for dumping your garbage. We tossed paper napkins, chip bags, empty cigarette packs, and spent butts out of car windows without a second thought. The interior of Ernie's 1957 Ford was spotless. "What are we, bums?" he'd holler. He liked it when we hurled pop bottles and Kleenex out the window to where they belonged.

Any pictures we took of "nature" were taken on summer driving trips to the States – distant mountains, or flat land stretching to the horizon with nothing on it except a single cactus or a motel sign.

Once we drove to Washington State to see the Grand Coulee Dam, which was advertised as the "Eighth Wonder of the World." I remember as a nine-year-old standing on the ridge of the dam and watching the span of water falling with a roar into the muddy Columbia River. Afterwards, Elsie said, "What makes that the Eighth Wonder of the World? It's just a lot of dirty water. I can look in a ditch at home and see the same thing."

My family was more interested in visiting the JCPenney store in Portland, Oregon. The towels and sheets you could buy there, they said, were out of this world. We loved these trips to the States. The Canadian dollar was worth more than the U.S. dollar. Everything was cheap, especially gas and motels, and we had amazing stories to tell when we returned. Steaks at the Frontier Restaurant in Wenatchee, Washington, the size of saddles! Free refills of coffee – everywhere!

As a kid I'd be stuck in the back seat between Elsie and Maudie with my bare legs sticking to the vinyl upholstery, hot air blasting from the open windows as we drove through another California desert heat wave. Up front, Ernie would be driving. My father, with the road map and a pencil behind his ear, would be acting as navigator, announcing the ETAs of whichever small town we were headed towards. Ernie and he wore identical blue-and-white ball caps and carried hand-kerchiefs in their short-sleeved pockets for wiping the sweat off their hands and foreheads. It was so hot in the desert that Elsie and Maudie rolled their stocking to their ankles and wore them like socks.

48

RITARDANDO

Dear Helen,

A few months ago, I heard the music of Arvo Pärt for the first time on the car radio as I drove through Sidney. It was a nine-minute piece for piano and violin called *Spiegel im Spiegel* (Mirror in the mirror), as I later found out. I also learned that Pärt was born in 1935 and is an Estonian composer of classical and religious music.

I imagine a gardener might have a similar experience to the one I had with Pärt's music. It happens when disparate events come together to produce a series of exquisite moments. An example might be watching a flock of sparrows alight from a tree at the same moment as the sun lights up a bank of Shasta daisies. At these times, you see things freshly, as if for the first time. You pause and hold your breath in wonder. In music, this pause is called a "ritardando."

What happened to me upon hearing *Spiegel im Spiegel* was that I began viewing the changing scene outside my car window in slow motion. Everything I saw became harmonious, filled with depth and intention.

It had been raining, but suddenly the sun broke through, hot. I noticed the steaming cars in the Save-On parking lot, their chrome bumpers flashing.

Looking for a place to park, I saw a heavy-set man leaning over the end of a pickup truck patting a wet golden retriever with a towel. Nearby, a middle-aged woman sat in the passenger's seat of a Smart car eating a chicken leg out of a cardboard container. Inside another car, a young man fumbled with a set of keys, trying to fit one into the ignition, while in the back seat, three small boys sat quietly, as if afraid. I saw an old man in a baseball cap sitting in the driver's seat of a beige sedan tapping the steering wheel with his fingers. Across the way, in the alcove by the bank, a group of teenage boys roughhoused while keeping an eye on the street, where an old woman with a walker held up traffic at the crosswalk.

On it went for nine minutes. Lives anonymous to one another, yet all of us included in this moving tableau, each of us unknowingly playing a part in the backdrop of another's life.

Nothing was more like life than what I was living in those moments.

Driving home, I turned off the radio. No music now, just the sounds of traffic, and the wind through the partially opened window. I took the winding road through the airport lands. The sun was fully shining, the rain clouds of only an hour before having disappeared.

In the fields on either side of the road cows usually grazed during the day. In the evenings they would regroup for the plodding journey alongside the road to the gate at the edge of the field. But this afternoon there were no cows to be seen. A man was striding through the tall grass. He was dark-haired and wore a brown suit jacket, reminding me of the character played by Harry Dean Stanton in the film *Paris, Texas*, a madman who strode through a similar field of grass. About to board a plane, this man had asked, incredulous, "You mean it leaves the ground?"

Later, at home, and still under the spell of Arvo Pärt's music, I sat on the back deck with a cup of tea. I became aware of the warm breeze getting stronger, of the warmth of the sun on my face. I watched a honeybee flying between swaying clematis leaves. A group of dragonflies passed by in a zigzag manner, as if travelling along some erratic stairway. I noticed the blue flash of their wings. Cloud stacks, grey on their undersides, hung above the Saanich Inlet.

49

EGGS

Dear Helen,

In last week's column, the one published before Christmas Day, you wrote about the nostalgia of the season, of its being linked to "conviviality and kindness expressed among family and friends and extended to others." You also wrote about revelling in "life's basics, such as simple quality food."

Arthur, along with his wife, Sharon, owns the ramshackle Cheerful Chicken Farm up the road. The farmyard includes machine parts arranged on outdoor tables beneath white plastic sheets serving as roofs, long rolls of tar paper piled here and there, pens for ducks and turkeys on the front grass, an outdoor fridge. The farmhouse itself is a typical suburban split-level house with a cathedral entrance, built in the eighties. The "free-run" chickens are kept out back in large moveable pens designed by Arthur. This is so they can follow the worms, he once told me.

Because of the extra people we were having over Christmas, I called him to ask for more eggs – more than my usual weekly dozen. He must have been feeling good that day because he said, "I have been put on the planet to make you happy! You can have half a dozen. You can have four. You can even have one egg to make a cake! Whatever you need. All you have to do is phone or email."

Arthur is in his sixties and somewhat eccentric. Besides being a full-time chicken farmer, he's also an engineer. The outdoor fridge, where he keeps customers' eggs, is rigged with a buzzer inside his house to alert him whenever the fridge door is opened. Then he promptly appears in his jeans, suspenders, and an old plaid shirt and says hello, has a chat, and collects the money. In this way, theft of the egg money, a problem in the area, is avoided. I often wonder if he sits on a stool inside the door waiting for the buzzer to ring.

He keeps track of egg sales on a computer spreadsheet and includes a cheery note with the summer eggs, reminding customers that the new crop of chickens isn't producing large eggs yet and that for a few weeks a dozen eggs will include some smaller sizes. He hopes we don't mind. No one minds. His eggs are the best anywhere; no one sells eggs with yolks more orange, or fresher, than Arthur does.

He also sells organic frozen chickens. One year I ordered an eight-pound bird for Thanksgiving and was assigned the bird's number, 372. For weeks before the pickup, I thought unceasingly about this bird – its singularity, its state of mind. What colour were its feathers? How old was it exactly? Did it wear a tag with the number 372 printed on it along with my name? It all became too intimate and when Terry took it out of the oven to carve at the table, I felt like I was about to eat a dear friend. I couldn't do it. I had the vegetables and stuffing instead.

I can count on the fingers of one hand the number of people who seem to have been put on the planet to make me happy.

50

WINTER GARDEN

Dear Helen,

Last week I stopped at Brett's vegetable stand down the road and was dismayed to find he'd closed for the winter. And, of course, he would close. It is early January, things have stopped growing, in particular the chard, spinach, broccoli, turnips, carrots, and tomatoes I've come to depend upon. His stand won't reopen until early spring.

One of your recent columns, Helen, was about growing a winter garden and what you call the "great treats" and "enormous pleasure" that the home gardener experiences at this time of year while pulling up carrots and beets. If there was ever a reason to grow vegetables during the winter months, here it is. I experienced no pleasure in finding that Brett's broccoli was no longer available, nor was it a great treat to later be picking over wilted chard at the grocery store.

Brett's father, that day, was sitting in his wheelchair in the weak afternoon sun and called me over. I walked to where he was seated near the stand. He said: "Here you are, a beautiful woman getting out of your car by yourself. There used to be a time when you wouldn't get out of a car unless I said you should. Things change, not that they shouldn't, but isn't it funny. Isn't change funny? I've been sitting here thinking about it and it's making me laugh."

This is something a Buddha would say. As I've already mentioned, Brett's father has dementia, and yet he's still finding things to laugh about. Or maybe in his dementia he's stumbled into a state of bliss and wisdom we could all use.

A definition of humour that I've come across has it being "a state of happy alertness." And this, certainly, is the way Brett's father seems to be every time I see him. He doesn't seem to feel solemn about anything. Unlike the rest of us, whose world of climate change and heavy-handed politics is getting a failing grade.

But as my climate-scientist friend, the writer Renée Hetherington, tells me, "The planet will be fine. It will correct itself. It will find a new state of equilibrium, whether by forming another Snowball Earth or reinstating a climate so warm that alligators will once again swim near the North Pole. Earth long ago developed a solution for a dominant species gone awry – extinction, in its fullest sense."

Why is this a weirdly comforting thought? Maybe it's the alligators swimming at the North Pole. Maybe it's our still-beautiful world carrying on without us.

It's unnatural to feel solemn all the time. What we want to hear about is joie de vivre, the whole-hearted love of whatever world we have left. We want to play and create, build our families and communities, continue to love one another, retain our sense of joy and astonishment about our own lives, our own beginnings. We want to hear that everything will somehow be fine.

If some of us are cheerleaders by being funny and silly and goofy and singing stupid songs, couldn't we think of this as service work?

51

DORMANT

Dear Helen,

During the winter months here in the Pacific Northwest, only the evergreens seem alive. The skies are leaden, the ground soggy from continual rain. Except for now, in mid-January, when it's frozen after a week of snow and subnormal temperatures. I took some seed outside just now for the birds and noticed the rainwater in the wheelbarrow had frozen, but that, so far, the daffodil shoots are still erect. The bamboo, which we have in several places around the yard, is holding up – in a haiku kind of way. I shook the snow from the branches. There is nothing else to be done in the yard now except to offer hope that the plants and birds survive.

Inside, I could read about the great gardeners of the past, but I won't. Or read about the manifold delights available to me by considering the plant's point of view, as suggested by Michael Pollan in his book *The Botany of Desire*. There is "a human desire that connects us to plants," he writes. But, somehow, I can't summon the energy (or the desire) to think about this. I'm off plants today. It's enough to drink my coffee and stare out the window. It's winter. We're not meant to garden in winter, and it's blowing snow again.

The sign outside the nearby nursery says "Gone Dormant." I'm feeling the same way. The nursery won't reopen for several weeks, and I probably won't, either. A "Special Weather Bulletin" on the Weather Network site today mentions "a series of disturbances," "outflow winds," and "a fair degree of uncertainty," which about describes my mood. It's the first winter I've ever felt so glum. If winter is a time of rest for plants, for many of us, with the short days and long nights, it's a time of brooding. I catch myself at the dinner table staring at the candle flames while a piece of potato cools on my fork.

Here's a definition for "dormant" that I've recently thought up: "Lying with head on hands, as if asleep, or almost dead."

52

TAUT

Dear Helen,

The mindfulness practitioners say the future will be just another set of present moments, so it's no big deal, nothing to worry about, nothing to fear; when the future arrives, it will be another "now," as whole and as perfect as you could want it to be, whatever form it takes. But they also say that if you aren't being mindful, the future could be a moment just as easily missed as this one, which is the thought I'm most partial to just now. Because what if you'd rather take a pass on a future that includes what you most fear: decrepitude, mindlessness, and loss? Assuming, of course, you get that far.

For me, worrying about personal ageing has been getting mixed up lately with worrying about the world.

"What do we do with knowledge that we cannot bear to live with, the knowledge that we do not want to know?" asks Deborah Levy in *Things I Don't Want to Know*.

Her answer? You don't faint. From a subsequent book, *The Cost of Living*, she clarifies this statement. The things you don't want to know "are the things that are already known to us but we don't want to look at closely." She suggests a person face up to the knowledge, understand that there is little you can do to change it, and move on, adding a further option: "Buy a bus ticket and travel all the way to acceptance."

John Gray, in *Straw Dogs*, noting our denial of the tragic, said this: "The good life is not found in dreams of progress, but in coping with tragic contingencies."

This, too, is the forward thinking of American ecophilosopher and scholar Joanna Macy, who suggests in her writings and workshops that there are ways we can cope with what is now happening in the world. A Buddhist, she offers what she calls her "four *R*s": "resilience, relinquishment, restoration, and reconciliation." All involve a coming together to determine what values and beliefs we want to hold onto, what we can let go of, what we want to bring forward from the past, and what we can do to make peace with what we have. All involve acceptance of "what is." She stresses practising gratitude, as well as asking open questions: "When I face the collapse of our whole culture, what I am grateful for is ..." And, "When I face the collapse of our world, what breaks my heart is ..."

My aunt Elsie's response to anything distressing – though, admittedly, she didn't have a collapsing world to worry over – was, "Quit being so bloody *morbid*. Do something useful."

Her solution was action, which, curiously, is Joanna Macy's solution, and many other people's, as well. Elsie remained "in action" well into her ninth decade, managing to live independently until the end, still keeping her fingers lodged in everyone's flesh. She died after making breaded veal cutlets for her supper on a Thursday night. She "took sick," as people used to say, and died in the hospital a few hours later.

"Remember March 31 is my birthday," she said when she was sixty and I was eighteen and leaving home for university in Vancouver. (She was not without a sense of humour.) "Because if you forget and don't visit with a present or, at the very least, make a phone call, I'm going to get drunk wearing that blue rag of a housecoat you hate so much, and then get lost down the beach, fall over a rotten log, and drown in the ocean. You will be sorry for the rest of your life."

Nevertheless, a doctor intervened at the crucial moment to announce that she'd died of old age at ninety-eight.

A week later there was the service at Sand's Funeral Home. Everyone in the family ended up there. Sand's was a long-estab-lished Victoria business. It was a tradition. When someone died, you called them up; you didn't have to think about where to go. Then you went to their showroom and picked out the coffin, set the date, and they took care of everything else.

For Ernie's service, we went into the Arbour Room with its light wood walls and hard, pew-like seats, and listened to a man no one knew officiating. He talked from notes about what a good man Ernie was, loyal, trustworthy, and so on, and that he'd built his own house, the Cordova Bay house, that he played the organ in his spare time, that he tended the boilers at the Victoria Public Library. It was over in five minutes.

Then, because the family were regular customers, we were driven in three long funeral cars to the graveside for the intern-ment. Getting into the cars, Ernie's sister, Stella, got put out, literally. She said she was supposed to be in the car with Billy and me, and two of Ernie's nephews, but there was no room. Her place had been taken by my new boyfriend, Mark. I don't know who assigned the seats – I'm guessing no one. But Mark didn't offer to get out of the car.

Stella was mad about this for years and told the story many times, and always with venom. She had a right as Ernie's sister, she said, to be in that car, and Mark, a stranger, had no right to have taken her place. Because there was no room in the other cars, she'd had to ride to the cemetery in her own car along with her peevish husband, Roy.

But she got her revenge on the family. Her dying wish – eight years later – was to be buried beside Ernie in his double plot on the green hillside of Royal Oak Burial Park. And she was. How this came about, I don't know. Elsie, then still alive, was bumped from her future use of the plot next to her husband in favour of Stella in the here and now. Many of us thought this was blackly funny at the time because Elsie had been a shrew with Ernie, and would he really have wanted to lie with her in eternal unrest?

So, this is how Elsie, who outlived Ernie by thirty-four years, came to be buried in a single plot in Hatley Memorial Gardens, which, as everyone knows, borders the busy road leading to Royal Roads Military College and is as far from any eternal rest imaginable.

As for a death in our family, there has always been someone to blame, someone to be angry at afterwards. Maybe all families do this. It's a vent, a need to replace our bewilderment and grief. It'll be the doctor, the bank manager, the funeral home director, the executor of the will, some hapless relative who said the wrong thing at the service, a neighbour who failed to send a condolence card. This blaming serves to unite the family at such times and is as necessary as oxygen.

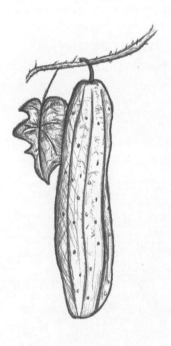

53

BONES

Dear Helen,

Your column today was about friends helping friends with food dishes when they're ill, and also what you, Helen, are eating these days – a Winter Luxury pumpkin made into a pie with a hazelnut crust, and salads made of carrots, beets, and radishes, all from your winter garden. These descriptions were coupled with a reminiscence about your time spent in Egypt during your "youthful travelling years" and discovering sugar cane at a street market, an ingredient you have used throughout your adult life.

I, too, have a standby ingredient that I've used over the years, thanks to my high-school home economics teacher, Miss Horel, though it wasn't "discovered" in the sense that your sugar cane was. Rather, its use was "imprinted" on me over a series of dull afternoon classes. I didn't realize it at the time, but she was handing her pupils one of the great secrets of the homemaker's art.

Miss Horel was all about thrift in the kitchen and making do with less and, though I hated the domesticity she preached at the time, I later followed much of what she taught. Because

141

of her lessons about home management, I can now manage just about anything, including, if necessary, a small country.

In 1963 she stood before her class of twenty fifteen-year-old girls at Claremont Secondary School in Cordova Bay, a massive woman – tall, with a large bosom and permed brown hair, inviolate in her handmade tweed suit with its handmade buttonholes.

Outside the classroom the sun shone, plum trees blossomed, and boyfriends waited for us in jazzed-up cars. It was the last period on a Friday afternoon and Miss Horel had important things to say to us about bones.

"There is no reason to go hungry in a civilization such as ours if you have a bone, a carrot, some salt and water, and a source of heat," she was saying. "Even a chewed bone will make good soup. Pork, lamb, beef, chicken, it doesn't matter."

We took notes. We all knew why we were there. We were housewives-in-training. Eventually, a perfected version of Miss Horel's soup would find its way into the slurping mouths of our shirt-and-tie husbands. By that time, the eternal source of life-giving heat would be ours: we'd have a man, a home, children, but, most importantly, a stove in a kitchen of our own.

"Substitute any other vegetable for the carrot," Miss Horel continued, "and you get the same result – a nourishing meal. And if no bones are available, used or otherwise, substitute rice, beans, lentils, or a can of vegetable soup. Season the soup with curry powder; it gets rid of the watery taste. Soup can last for days."

Because it was close to Saint Patrick's Day, she said, "Besides potatoes, the nineteenth-century Irish lived on Scotch broth, which is lamb bones and barley soup flavoured with one shrivelled carrot and a dried-out onion scavenged from the back of the broom closet."

"It's always fascinated me," she carried on, "why so many people get excited on Saint Patrick's Day about the life of a Catholic priest, who traipsed around ancient Ireland banishing snakes and converting people to Christianity. You can't do a thing with snake meat."

"Snake meat," we wrote. "Saint Patrick." "Shrivelled carrot."

Soup-making was important work, she told us, and a vital skill to have if we wanted to take our places as confident home-makers of the nation.

"Cruel and unusual punishment" was what my friends and I called home ec. But, as it turned out, knowing how to make soup has been a good thing. Once, during hard times in the eighties, it actually was chewed steak bones that I boiled up for my family, adding carrots and an onion, as per Miss Horel's instructions.

54

NIGHT WALK

Dear Helen,

The day before my father died, he asked me, "Are you prepared?" I didn't know what to make of the question. I was six months pregnant and sitting at his bedside at the Royal Jubilee Hospital in Victoria. He had lung cancer. He'd smoked for sixty years, and quit the day he was admitted to hospital, which was two weeks earlier. Be prepared? Was he telling me I should be prepared, like a Girl Guide? Prepared for the birth of my daughter? Prepared for his coming death? Prepared for the consequences of smoking cigarettes? Should I be thinking of taking up the habit? Prepared for what? Decades later, I am still asking the question. For what?

He had a sense of humour. Maybe that was it. Was he giving me some final, koan-like words to last my lifetime? He liked to say the opposite of what you expected him to say. He liked irony and wit. When I passed grade six, he sent me five dollars in a letter that began, "The Bored of Education is so pleased ..." When I passed the Royal Conservatory piano exam for grade three, he signed the congratulatory letter, "From Major C."

After he died, I found a note in his wallet about stopping his health insurance: "In the event of my demise ..." it began. I thought this was funny because it sounded as if he thought his "demise" was unlikely – ever. Then I understood that "demise" was one of those veiling words.

His funeral was modest. Reverend Robert Samson, who married Terry and me, conducted the service, held in the Garden Chapel at Sands Funeral Home in Victoria. There was a casket, flowers, tea and coffee in a room at the funeral "home," but no graveside service.

Still, I felt his life needed a greater tribute, and this is something I have done for him ever since, in my daily life, and in several of my books. Bill is named after him. Anna has Gibson as a middle name. And now our grandson has Gibson as his first name, though his second name, Gale, is what he's called by. My point being that when you have only one parent, and that parent (and grandparent) is a good one, you triple up on appreciation.

The American writer David Markson, in his later novels, catalogued the end of many artists' lives – to addictions, disease, accident, abandonment, suicide. These books were lists of one death after another interspersed with interesting facts about a notable's life, sometimes wryly observed, but always given as a bald statement. Strangely, the books are mesmerizing to read.

And there was Markson himself in 2007, writing in *The Last Novel*, his last work, that he, as the narrator, was "Old. Sick. Tired. Alone. Broke." He said that several times during the course of the book. Did he find comfort, if not pleasure, in cataloguing with a few details that even the most revered and admired among us must one day die? Markson himself had been dead for two days in 2010 before he was found sitting up in bed.

He was eighty-two years old. He'd been ignored as a writer until his later years. Did this late recognition act as a consolation prize during his final moments?

Because of his writing about other people's deaths, I've often wondered what, exactly, his own was like. The state of his bedroom, for example, which I'm guessing would be a mess, with books, papers, and index cards strewn about; the bed covers rumpled and in need of a wash; mugs, dirty plates, and pill bottles crowded together on the bedside table. What facts about David Markson could be memorialized? His own: "Old, sick, tired, alone, and broke"? Or should they be even briefer? For the painter Jean-Michel Basquiat, Markson wrote that he "died of a heroin overdose. At twenty-seven." A life reduced to a couple of facts. But two facts, if you want to be remembered, are better than none, I suppose. Markson gave himself five, with uncharacteristic, though understandable, generosity. Ultimately though, who wants to keep count?

I was thinking these things as Terry and I prepared for our walk the other night, a walk I love to take in winter. It's an activity that renders me mindless; thoughts disappear, sensations arrive. Elsie would approve.

We encounter few cars when we're out, and often hear owls in the nearby woods, or Ray's chirps, if he decides to follow us. On a clear night there are stars. Even in rain, the air feels brisk.

I like turning off the flashlight and waiting for my eyes to adjust to the darkness. Trees disappear almost entirely. The familiar neighbourhood houses become blocks of shadow, outlined by still-hanging strings of Christmas lights. We seem to float as we walk along.

If life, as the Taoists have it, is a dream endlessly repeated, then this fragment of the dream, this night walk, has much to recommend it.

55

BIG SNOW

Dear Helen,

How are you getting on in the snow? We've been having a few days of "real winter," haven't we? I realize it's laughable to anyone east of Vancouver for us to be making such a big deal about it, but it's a rare event in our otherwise mild climate, and a little exciting. Were you snowed in? We were – for a day.

When the roads were finally cleared, I made the trip into Sidney for supplies – food, mainly, and candles. Traffic in Sidney was frantic. Everyone, it seemed, was sharing the same survivalist mentality I was.

So there I was, standing with my cart in a lineup at Thrifty Foods, third from the #5 till two days after the big snow. The place was bumper-to-bumper with carts along the aisles and at the tills. I had to pee but that wouldn't be happening any time soon because my line was a slow one. It would be a while before I got out of there.

An old guy, in the number one position ahead of me, was asking the cashier too many questions about the flyer. He thought beets and cat food were on sale. It was taking the cashier a while to convince him otherwise. Then he started helping her pack, and she was having to unpack because he put too many cans in one bag and wouldn't be able to lift it. Then he went on about the snow, giving her a weather report. "Two feet of the blasted stuff, and more coming! Going to be −4 tonight. Windchill of −11. Arctic outflow from the north. Ferries cancelled. Oh, we're in for it!" He seemed delighted, but I thought, "Will he never be done?"

The couple ahead of me would be having sausages for supper, I decided, also a tub of margarine, orange juice, and a bag of frozen French fries. Their groceries were already on the conveyer belt awaiting take-off. I always look at what groceries people buy. It's what you do while waiting in line. It's a form of clairvoyance. How long will the couple live on this diet, you wonder? He had a stoop; she had a bald spot at the crown of her head and her face was flushed. I put them in their late sixties. They were each about twenty pounds overweight. I gave them five more good years before the slide began.

I wasn't doing so well that day either, what with my impulse purchase of stew meat, even if it was organic. I'd hidden it under a bag of spinach, three oranges, and a bag of almonds. I thought if I was lucky only the cashier would see the meat. Is there such a thing as a confidentiality code with cashiers, like there is with doctors, lawyers, and priests?

I'd been thinking that stew would be a good thing to have on a cold winter's night. But how many times of eating red meat does it take to reduce a person's longevity? I wondered if eating spinach would cancel out that number. Or almonds. Panicked, I decided that this would be my last purchase of red meat ever. I would never eat it again. This move might be good for a couple of extra years.

I looked around. A woman waiting with her cart in the lineup across from me at the #6 till was applying lip liner and then lipstick, free standing, without a mirror. She was taking a long, careful time to do this. She had on red suede boots but was otherwise dressed in black. She looked chic. She caught my eye, left her line, and came towards me.

It was Julie-Ann. We'd been in the same spin class twenty years ago. Back then she hurled herself through a floor-length window one night because of some problem with her second husband and so missed a month of classes. But this day in Thrifty's she was smiling. Her lipstick was perfect. She wanted to ask me about writing instructors.

"I went to Heidi a few times, but she's stopped teaching," she said. "You know her? No? Well, I'm desperate. I really need to find a new instructor. I have so much to say. I need to get it down before it's too late."

Julie-Ann's line moved forward and she hurried back. The couple with the sausages was finally at the till. It wouldn't be long before they'd be frying them up, I thought, chugging down artery-clogging grease. It wouldn't be long before I'd get to leave with my life-shortening meat and find a bathroom. There were now five carts in my line.

I turned to the skinny young guy behind me to say something cheerful, like "Moving forward at last!" but he was working his phone. I noticed his cart contained nothing but fruit, vegetables, a sack of rice, and a large bag of split peas from the bulk bins. Another sixty years for him, I thought.

56

SEED CATALOGUE

Dear Helen,

I know you've been reading a lot of seed catalogues lately – and planning your garden for the coming season – because you've spoken about this several times in recent columns.

And so, when the *West Coast Seeds Gardening Guide* arrived in the mail last December, I dutifully had a look at it. I'd never read a seed catalogue before and expected it to be an exercise in dullness. But it wasn't long before I was feeling amazed. Are all seed catalogues like this one? Touching on the transcendent? It has a reach well beyond that of a mere sales vehicle. What makes this so is that it's filled with energetic wordplay in the descriptions of the vegetable, fruit, flower, and herb seeds on offer. Each seed description presents a vision of tomorrow. Each stage of the maturing seed promises to become a months-long lyric poem. The catalogue seems dedicated to lifting a gardener's heart.

Seduction by a seed catalogue. Seduced by a picture of a pea. The manifold delights available when considering the desire of a plant, the plant's point of view, the reciprocal relationship between plant and plant. These notions are found in Michael Pollan's *Botany of Desire*.

The West Coast Seeds catalogue has a friendly, earthbound consciousness about it as well, with anchoring sections on seed rotation projects, biodiversity, and a full explanatory page called "Soil Science 101." I felt especially warmed by the introductory note on page one. It wishes readers "a fantastic growing season full of joyful moments." I have never before been wished this at the start of reading anything.

The catalogue runs to one hundred and fifty-two pages, or one hundred and fifty-two potentially exquisite moments if you read it from end to end. It includes, besides seed descriptions, colour photographs, planting guides, regional charts, notes on garden pests, and a scintillating index that includes recipes for edamame and soil blockers, which, it turns out, are not something that stops soil from being soil, as I imagined, but a recipe for the special soil to be used in those little "blocks" to plant single seeds.

The expository writing, throughout, is factual and clear. But it's the language used for the seeds, especially for those of the vegetables and fruits, that delights.

Within the pages you will find Swiss chard that has "hot pink stocks," and strawberries with "rose-coloured flowers held aloft above glossy green foliage." Sides of the Hungarian cheese blend peppers are described as "flattened and fluted." Ruby grass is given a dramatic narrative: "In midsummer, the flowering stalks begin to appear, starting red, but fading to pink and then to creamy silver at maturity." Yes, I can see it. It's the lifecycle of myself and my friends.

The names of the seeds range from the prosaic to the cavalier to the astonished. "Golden Pearls," "Yellow Wonder," "Sugar Baby," which are all fruits. There's a shallot called "Ambition" and a radish called "White Icicle." An asparagus is named "Voltaire"; a cauliflower, "Sky Walker"; a lettuce, "Pomegranate Crunch."

Another is the playful "Jester Lettuce," described as having "flashy red speckles on semi-savoyed leaves," the word "savoyed" making the lettuce sound stylish. But "savoyed," when applied to a lettuce, I discovered, means it has a leaf that is abnormally curled and wrinkled. That's the jest of it; it's a surprise of a lettuce, one contrary to expectations.

Enthusiastic language is used, then, in the service of selling seeds. It's language that is emotional, meant to excite the gardener over a long-haul winter with the promise of brighter days to come. A language of hope.

If the catalogue were compared, say, to a book of contemporary poetry, whose language is often spare – "Never use more than one adjective at a time" is the usual directive in writing classes – the West Coast Seeds catalogue would be the place to find adjectives and adverbs run amuck. It's an English country garden full of pink and yellow words. It's also the place where, as in poems, "flesh" often reigns: "mild and crunchy" (radish), "tender, crisp, white" (also radish), "tart but never bitter" (rhubarb), "egg-yolk golden skin" (tomato), "tasty sweet tendrils" (zucchini).

I wondered who wrote the copy for the catalogue and so phoned the 1-888 number listed on the catalogue's back cover. It turns out to be one person, Mark Macdonald. He's been the catalogue writer for ten years, and has a "semi-literary" background, as he calls it, having published a pair of books in the early 2000s with Arsenal Pulp Press of Vancouver – a novel, *Flat*, and a story collection, *Home*. With the catalogue, he tries, he says, to write descriptions that are "sensual and emotional," and uses sentences that are full sentences, as opposed to the fragments that many of the catalogue's competitors use.

I can see why gardeners fall in love with this catalogue. It's all there – charged language, stunning pictures, the promise of tomorrow.

The print run for the yearly spring edition is 140,000 copies. Pitted against the average one-time print run of a Canadian book of poems, which is five hundred copies, this is an astounding fact. If only poetry could receive the same exposure.

Unlike literary books, there are no book launches for the West Coast Seeds catalogue, no appearances at festivals, no anxious self-promotions, no reading events held in libraries and church basements that only a handful of people attend. Launches and readings are not needed. The catalogue is delivered free of charge to thousands of adoring customers via Canada Post at the start of each winter season. As inspirational reading, seed catalogues get many of us through the darkest days of winter.

57

GLORY

Dear Helen,

It was a nightmare. I was required to appear before a jury of professional seed growers and talk about what I had done in the garden that day. There was a large audience in attendance. I had done nothing in the garden and so had to make things up. But whatever I said, people ran for the exits. My lying descriptions of working intimately with carrots and kale, my heated comments about worms, were apparently not convincing.

I was also required to show enthusiasm for the project I was working on – how to quit regarding the future with panic – and to field questions and listen to comments.

Not one ounce of me wanted to be standing before this jury, but, as it was a nightmare, I had no choice. I experienced the usual anguish throughout because I couldn't find my notes about the twenty-three varieties of sunflowers I thought would be of interest, and when I found the notes, they were written in chemical formulas, which I couldn't read, a typical nightmare scenario which has also become a typical description of the future – inexplicable.

There was only one comment from the jury. A woman in a beekeeper's hat said: "Why don't you sing us a song, Marion? Songs help a lot of people through tough times."

"I'm doing the best I can," I said, and wept.

"Hope, real hope, names the bitter reality before us. But it refuses to succumb, despite the bleakness, to despair." This is from a February 2020 Truthdig article by the author and journalist Chris Hedges, with the title "America: Land of Make-Believe."

How do we not succumb to despair about the times we are living through? How do we accept the "bitter reality" Hedges writes about? How do we not lose heart?

Perhaps the question needs to be reframed: "Why would we want to give up, admit defeat, cease resisting? Are there not our children and grandchildren to consider, our friends and communities? Why would we abandon them?"

Poet Seamus Heaney speaks of our need to listen to the "music of what happens." He says that only by attending to the most mundane sounds can the rare music of our souls be heard. Or, as Christian Wiman puts it, in *My Bright Abyss*: "To be truly alive is to feel one's ultimate existence within one's daily existence."

I am taking both these thoughts under advisement. If our lives, as I see it, are a combination of breath, and panic, and glory, I will acknowledge the panic, but try not to let it overtake me. Instead, I will seek equilibrium, giving shared billing to the glory part.

If only I could wake up.

58

SNAPDRAGONS

Seeding dwarf snapdragons indoors for an early-spring showing was the subject of your column today, Helen. They're among the first flowers to bloom in spring, you wrote, and seeding can start in late January and continue throughout February. The picture that accompanies the column is a closeup of two red-and-white snapdragons from a planter of yours taken during the previous season. I hadn't realized that most, if not all, of the photos accompanying your columns are taken by you. Nor had I realized what the name "snapdragon" means. It's a fanciful description of the flower's face, which has two parts like a mouth – a dragon's mouth.

But I won't be seeding snapdragons. I've decided that the one good thing I will grow this year will be the Crystal Apple cucumber. It's the vegetable from the first of your columns that I read and the one that started me on this ... what? This quest for calm abidance, for a way forward.

I've ordered the seeds from West Coast Seeds. The online site lists a lot of complicated growing instructions for cucumbers. It now seems such a forbidding task, and I'm feeling a little uneasy. Growing the Crystal Apple cucumber appears to be more complicated than caring for a dog or a cat. There are five-gallon containers to buy for the deck planting, and stakes that the cucumbers will need. There's the necessity of "hot" soil (what is that?) and special fertilizer, and worry over aphids and powdery mildew, which, it seems, cucumbers are susceptible to. Worst of all, there's the fact that some of the Crystal Apple cucumbers could shrivel on the vine and die. Shrivel and die. I'm already imagining that.

But I will prevail. For the delight and the jest of it, I will repeat this intention: A fantastic growing season is ahead, one that will be full of joy at the maturity of my chosen crop.

Meanwhile, I'll be listening for the music from that thing we are too self-conscious of and embarrassed to mention these days – the soul.

59

PARSLEY

Dear Helen,

Because growing the Crystal Apple cucumber is going to be a challenge and there's a good chance I might fail, I've decided to add another plant to my gardening plan for the coming spring, something simple and manageable, as you've advised in a recent column.

Parsley, it seems to me, represents both of these things. It should be easy to grow, shouldn't it? How could anyone fail with parsley, other than by not watering it? I'll admit it's probably a stupidly simple thing to grow, but I'm aiming for at least one guaranteed success. I'm stacking the deck, so to speak. Parsley will be my fallback "one good thing," my psychological insurance.

And I always need parsley for soups, stews, and fish, and otherwise I'll never have it fresh.

My choice of parsley has nothing to do, by the way, with the drippy Simon & Garfunkel song "Scarborough Fair," and the line "Parsley, sage, rosemary, and thyme," and everything to do with the perceived ease of the task, and of starting on a heartfelt level. Historically, parsley has been thought to stimulate sexual desire or "lust," as well as to attract money. So maybe ...

My parsley choice is described in the seed catalogue as having "big clusters of highly curled, dark-green leaves" and of being "wonderful" in Mediterranean and Middle Eastern dishes.

Can you see it? Parsley growing lustfully in a pot on the deck.

The seed catalogue says mid-April is the time to seed parsley which, I've just learned, is classified as an herb. (My ignorance must astound you!) This gives me enough time to research the growing requirements and order my choice of seed, Forest Green parsley. It's the variety that's most common and is often used as a garnish.

Seeding parsley will be an ordinary thing, properly done.

60

BOUNTY

Dear Helen,

One of my favourite books as a young mother was *Preserving Summer's Bounty* by Marilyn Kluger. It contains sections on freezing, drying, and storing garden produce, and recipes for making jams and pickles, as well as practical how-to advice about canning fruits and vegetables. But I found the best part of the book to be Kluger's vignettes about growing up on a farm in the American Midwest during the Great Depression of the 1930s.

    Published in the late seventies, the book became something of a back-to-basics motivator for many of my generation, and, for a while, I became an enthusiastic practitioner. Chapter titles included "Grandmother's Mincemeat," "Grandpa's Outdoor Cellar," and "Preserving Fruits in Spirituous Liquids," and each chapter had a story to tell. I rhapsodized over sentences like: "The kitchen table was a veritable cornucopia for the harvest; in the centre, piled in a crunchy mound on the ironstone meat platter, might be quail Dad had hunted, or smoky fried ham slices cut from the muslin-shrouded ham that hung in the smokehouse."

Kruger's vignettes, read by me nearly fifty years after the events it describes, represented a fantasy. I knew this at the time. But the happy farm family stories she told alongside her recipes, and which showcased a family working together to achieve what we now call sustainability, were seductive. Hers was a picture of a domestic golden age, and, even though it was the Depression, her family, she wrote, "lived like the wealthy" because they grew and shot everything they needed to survive.

For me, "going back to basics" took the form of making my own bread. Suddenly, the denatured bread that had sustained us through our growing-up years (Wonder Bread) was considered dangerous, even life-threatening.

In my quest for an alternative, I scoured Victoria until I found a supply of whole-wheat grain from the Church of Jesus Christ of Latter-day Saints, also known as the Mormons. This was in 1982, when there were few health food stores about. I ground the wheat – organic Winter Red brought to Vancouver Island from Saskatchewan on a train car and then by barge via the church congregation – in my new wood-framed wheat grinder. I bought the grinder at considerable expense, also from the church, an organization with a survivalist bent; each family has a year's supply of food on hand in case of disaster and/or the breakdown of civilization as we know it. My friends and I, like the Mormons, were convinced that this breakdown was inevitable. Singing along at one of our herb-tea-and-banana-loaf gatherings to Jackson Browne's "Before the Deluge" – "the brave and crazy wings of youth ..." – everyone was so *moved*.

It seems amusing, even absurd, now. But worry about societal breakdown is, of course, once again with us.

Elsie, who was from the generation that loved labour-saving devices, instant food, and lethal cleaning products, was confused by my new-found domestic zeal.

"Why would you want all that work?" she asked. "Your grandmother had all that work but she had no choice. There was no such thing as instant rice or frozen pizza in her day. She made everything from scratch, sewed and knit our clothes, and even boiled water on a wood stove to do her washing. She was a wreck. She never had a minute to herself."

For a while, I inhabited a nostalgia for what I believed to be a richer and simpler time. It was like living in a pop-up theme park, one seriously divorced from the reality of our daily lives in the eighties, which included fear of nuclear war, child-rearing, and worries about money. I donned the wholesome "can-do" values like a housewife's apron, but it didn't last long.

My mania for living like Kluger evaporated the day I spent six hours with forty pounds of hard-skinned apples and managed to produce only three tiny jars of jelly.

That was when I re-entered the world of complexities, realizing I'd been play-acting. But then another mania resurfaced, one that had been smouldering since high school – writing.

61

RESILIENCE

Dear Helen,

"A long hard winter lived through from beginning to end without shirking is one of the most salutary experiences in the world. There is no nonsense about it; you could not indulge in vapours and the finer sentiments if you tried." So wrote Elizabeth von Arnim in the 1890s in *The Solitary Summer.*

And now winter here is almost over. The finer sentiments – but not the "vapours" von Arnim speaks of, which I take to be the toxic airs of depression – are gathering on the horizon with their exclamation marks of awe and their capital letters of praise. Soon, flowering daffodils, the early blooms of the *Clematis armandii* and blossoming cherry trees, will be a feature of daily life and we will be swooning.

Your column today featured a plant that has, you wrote, an "utterly undemanding resilience," one that's survived the snow and rain and windstorms of winter. It's called the catchfly, and has "thick clusters of nodding rosy-pink blooms." I had to look up the variety as I'm unfamiliar with it. It turns out to be (forgive me – I'm sure you know) a variety of Sweet William, a perennial, the flowers ranging from pink to purple to orange. Attached to the description of this plant are the gardening words I love: "Pest-free, low maintenance, drought-tolerant."

What a cheerful thing it would be to see purple catchfly in the garden in mid-February. My daffodils are now showing plump buds through their skins and the hellebore in the pot on the front steps beginning to show its white-green blooms, but that's all the colour we have in the yard so far. The coming week of sun that's now forecast, after two months of steady rain and that week of snow, should help things along.

Thanks to you and your columns, I've been taking the time to notice what is especially beautiful at this time of the year – the growth that's occurring beyond our gardens, in forests, boulevards, and laneways. Many of the red-stemmed wild willows are now in leaf, as is the ocean spray, a shrub apparently common to the wild parts of the Pacific Northwest. It will bloom in May, with tiny white flowers arranged on long tendrils. Ocean spray is another resilient species, and I'm informed it's often the first plant to surface in a burned-out area or a clear-cut.

For me, what before had been a casual appreciation of the native plants near my home has now become an exercise in noticing. I've seen these plants all my life but, for many of them, I never asked the questions: What is it called? What is the species? What is its growing season? Is it native to our part of the world?

On this morning's walk, which was chilly, though bright, I noticed the mosses. The new, vividly green growth has begun appearing on the sides of tree trunks and branches that line the trail to Warrior Point. And there's another variety of moss that drapes itself over branches, hanging down in a ghostly fashion, like a pale-green shawl.

The interesting part about this trail is the way the plant species change as we walk along. To begin, there's a ground cover of ivy, blackberry vines, sword ferns, wild huckleberry, and invasive daphne. But this changes to salal, Oregon grape, and red-stemmed willow the nearer the trail gets to the Point, and the beach at Pat Bay. All these plants have a resilience that is beyond question.

"God is in the details," as architects say, a phrase that could be applied not only to buildings and art, but to forest walks. This morning, noticing the many varieties of plant life served to deepen my walking pleasure. Once again, the gravitational pull of beauty in the natural world was performing its magic. For me, it's become a pull that's stronger than the pull of an online shopping site or a news clip about impending doom.

62

GLEE

Dear Helen,

Your headline today was uplifting. "Dry Weather Brings a Glee-ful Return to Garden Work." It's the word "gleeful" that caught my attention. After a period of "incessant rain and gloom," you wrote, "re-entry" into the garden was a cause for celebration.

Commenting on the many things that needed your attention – preparing plots, tidying, pruning, hauling – you said, "It's easy to become entirely absorbed in work like this. The rest of the world and its many problems disappear."

I've read something else like this recently. It was about finding the transcendent state of grace in the hard reality of daily living (Christian Wiman, *My Bright Abyss*). Surely, absorption in gardening work would qualify as a state of grace. A quote you use in the column is from a book, *A Garden at My Door* by Cicely Wylie, given to you by your New Zealand aunt many years ago and seems to confirm this idea: "Gardening is one of the joys in life. To many of us, it offers a refuge, remote from much that is ugly in the world today."

The *Merriam-Webster.com Dictionary* is not without humour when it comes to giving examples of "refuge" (shelter, sanctuary): "Religion may be a refuge from the woes of your life; a beautiful park may be a refuge from the noise of the city; and your bedroom may be a refuge from the madness of your family."

In one grand sweep, we travel from religion to the noise of business to the madness of families. There are so many novels written about the latter. Contradicting Tolstoy's famous opening sentence in *Anna Karenina* – "Happy families are all alike ..." – I would contend, instead, that it's unhappy families who are all alike. It's happy families that apparently are a rare breed, that seem more complex and mysterious, worthy of attention. How do they do it? How do they keep the balls of happiness in the air? How do they tip the balance from the presumed discord, despair, and "madness" of unhappy families towards one that isn't predominately unhappy?

But to return to the matter of "glee," which you said you experienced upon returning to work in your garden. I'm imaging it was the "laughing song and merriment" sort of glee found in a Gilbert and Sullivan operetta. A transporting, high-spirited joy. What a reliable thing a garden can be in the gaiety department, as you indicate in your column. It's the place you can keep returning to and receive, more often than not, this blast of high emotion. Our neighbour, who works at a busy medical clinic, has started raising chickens in her backyard. She says the happiness factor of doing this is huge for her. She loves cleaning the pens, feeding the chickens, collecting eggs, worrying over them, pulling on her mucky boots, her old jacket, and spending an hour each day with them in the coop. Chicken care is her refuge.

The purest form of glee, to my mind, can be found in small children. Their glee is radiant, transparent, fully confident, unselfconscious. We've all seen this.

It was in full play when we took our three-year-old grand-daughter Flynne to Mayfair Mall on a rainy Monday afternoon in late January. After lunch in the food court, we roamed through the bright white thoroughfare. She soon took off her coat and ran freely, like an off-leash dog, before sitting on every available sofa chair that was part of the "living room" arrangements outside the stores for use by mall customers.

Then Flynne noticed the mannequins in the store window of Garage Clothing. There were five of them made of grey plastic, all without heads or feet. Each one was wearing a long white T-shirt with red lettering across their female chests that said "SALE." The stub ends of the mannequin's legs were shoved into a lattice of rough wood. Flynne thought they were funny, and I was relieved. This meant that headless, footless figures probably wouldn't reappear to her later as a nightmare.

I took her into the Roots store where she could see other mannequins, ones without lower bodies but that had heads with no faces. In place of a face there was a flat, white, oval surface, like the side of an egg. These mannequins were dressed in jackets and various wool hats. One was of a child, wearing an orange toque, which Flynne again found funny. An older saleswoman smiled at us indulgently.

From there, we made an anthropological expedition of it. I told her that mannequins were made of plastic and explained what plastic was. Then I gave her a brief lesson about commerce, telling her mannequins existed only to sell clothes; they were like dressed-up dolls; you could change their clothes depending on what you were selling. She liked this idea. I also told her it was a good thing to notice what was in her immediate surroundings, external to herself. But of course this is something I now remember that three-year-olds do naturally.

We next went into the La Senza lingerie store. "Senza" means "without" in Italian, I told her. Here, all the mannequins were torsos, without arms, legs, or heads, and were not dressed with *clothes*, except for bras and underwear. The plastic of these mannequins was coloured black. They were high up and hung from the walls like statues of bizarre saints in a Dadaist church. Flynne liked the colours of the underwear but was otherwise unimpressed with the torsos.

In Reitmans Flynne touched a mannequin's bone-white hand and kept repeating the word "plastic," which was a new word for her, as was "mannequin." She spent a few moments examining the mannequin's fingers, which were lifelike and included the semblance of nails. This mannequin was wearing jeans and a slouchy blue sweater but did not have a head or feet.

The mannequins excited Flynne so much that she wanted to enter more stores to catalogue the different types. At each store, she would call out loudly: "No head!" "No legs!" It was as if we were birders, but instead of long hushed waits for a sighting, we were overwhelmed with an abundance of our chosen quarry and had to rush about to see them all. She found our cataloguing delightful, as did I, and would pull my hand urgently and say, "Come on, Grandma!" to enter another store.

"I like them," she said a while later from my lap. We were resting on one of the mall's chairs, placed two feet away from a TV screen showing a men's basketball game. She liked the mannequins as opposed to the octopus she'd seen the day before at the aquarium. She hadn't liked the moving tentacles.

There is nothing more beautiful than the state of grace that laughter brings.

EPIC POTATOES

Dear Helen,

This day is about driving through the archway of cherry blossoms on Third Street leading into Sidney and seeing a woman in a pink dressing gown sitting on her front steps smoking a cigarette, and how the colour of her dressing gown matched those cherry blossoms exactly.

It's about there being an early gasp of spring in the air, with the sun being out, and King Alfred daffodils, blossoming heathers and crocuses growing in front yards and boulevards.

It's also about my visit to the grocery store where I overheard a middle-aged couple talking beside the pickle jars. I was further up the aisle deciding which brand of mustard to buy.

The man said, "I don't like these jokes, dear."

And the woman said, "Hey, every bit counts!"

I didn't catch their joke, but I noticed her – frizzy hair, white leather jacket with fringe – while he was a short blur. Later, when they were behind me in the checkout line, I looked in their shopping cart and saw it was full of supplies for the pandemic – salt-and-vinegar chips, Diet Coke, Lysol, protein bars, potatoes.

A short while later, the woman said, "Shit! I forgot the epic poems!" And the man said, "Jesus, Cindy, that's not even funny."

As a result of hearing this conversation, my day became one of thinking about epic poems, those ancient verse narratives of a time beyond living memory: tales of heroic men and women dealing with gods and supernatural forces; mythical stories about evil; the battles to shape a moral universe and the hero's trials in doing this. I thought of the *Odyssey*, the *Iliad*, the *Epic of Gilgamesh*, the Bible, and even *Game of Thrones*, which could also be called an epic with its fantastic villains, creatures, and warring peoples.

I continued on this line of thinking while having coffee in the Bevan Bistro with three friends and, as a result, barely heard their conversation, which turned out to be about planting potato tubers in their vegetable gardens. They mentioned they'd read your column this morning – "If Space Is Limited, Choose High-Yielding Potatoes" – which was about the muddy-red coloured potatoes called Ama Rosa. My friend Nancy said she was giving her full consideration to planting this "epic potato" come spring.

Soon after, the gardening conversation petered out and moved towards one of the main subjects of all epic poems – death. This is something I've noticed that conversations are doing a lot these days, sliding in this direction. It's as if we've lost control over them – as if they've evolved into separate life forms with wills of their own. You say to a person, "Have you seen the blossoms on Third Street?" And the reply will be, "Yes, but have you seen today's death count?"

Then I overheard a woman at the next table say, "Most birds can talk if they are taught. They're just like us. Wouldn't you agree? We are all kin in the story of evolution. But we have drifted far from it due to that God myth."

This statement further contributed to my thinking about epic poems. Because isn't what we are living through now, with this novel virus, epic poem material? One day, we woke up and discovered we were right in the middle of a battle, which is the way epic poems usually begin, in the middle of the trial, and at the hero's lowest point. Weren't we now at our "lowest point"? Scared, "sheltering in place," engaged in a terrifying battle with an invisible enemy, not knowing the outcome – and all the while experiencing time differently, the usual flow of it seeming to have stopped, or at least paused. Time having become otherworldly, like a dream.

I'd had a dream a few nights before, I suddenly remembered, in which my friend Jane asked me to write an epic poem she could use on her CV. She wanted to impress an interview panel. In dream-speak language that I understood perfectly, she said, "If you do this for me, Marion, I promise I will give you a broom to sweep the epic poem and everything else into God's great pot."

There was "that God myth" again. Which returned me to Cindy in the grocery store and wondering what you can buy there that sounds like "epic poem." Had I misheard her? I couldn't think of anything and began to wonder if Cindy was actually saying some brilliant and comic thing: that she'd nailed the zeitgeist about where we are in the world, which was living inside an epic poem.

This was when the camera of the omniscient narrator pulled back from the Bevan Bistro for a bird's-eye view of the town of Sidney and the cherry blossoms on Third Street below. A further pullback revealed a satellite view of Vancouver Island, which was seen as a tiny green thing the size of a snail floating off the northwest coast of North America. You couldn't see any of us, not on the Island, not on North America. We had become invisible beneath the canopy of beige and green. Finally, the camera crashed through the spring sky and headed for the darkness beyond. This is the place in some epic poems where you will find God's great pot. But it's also the place where you will not find a single human molecule.

FLIES

Dear Helen,

Since many things are shutting down now because of the COVID-19 virus, I thought your column might be shutting down, as well. But no! There it was this morning alongside a bright picture of blueberries on the vine. Your headline read, "Traps Help Curb Spotted-Wing Drosophila." It made me glad to see it.

Your column was shorter than usual, perhaps because the newspaper is slimmer. Many sports events and performances are cancelled, so there's less for the paper to report on. But brief as your column was, your answer to D.B. about the "fairly new" fruit fly to the region that is playing havoc with summer berries and your suggestions about how to trap and destroy them was, once again, a welcome antidote for me to fearful thinking.

Because I've been finding myself sentimental for what we had just a short while ago: the delicious oblivion about what was to come. "Back then," we didn't have "social distancing," "flattening the curve," "states of emergency," "lockdowns," "self-isolation" – new states of being that we are now shakily inhabiting. We didn't have "catastrophic surges" or daily "death tolls."

D.B. must have been asking her question about white worms weeks or months ago, before any of this started. It seems hysterical now to think of her, me, all of us, worrying over such a thing as a white worm infestation when pitted against a pandemic. But this is precisely what we need to be thinking about. The world isn't over. We are not over. And, happily, the annoying worms are not over. They, it turns out, are larvae from the spotted-wing drosophila, which is a fly. I read your straightforward answer to D.B. with tremendous appreciation. Calm abidance in action!

We are fortunate to shelter here in a place that is not densely populated, which means that going for long walks in the open air is a possibility. Today, we saw our friend Phil in his yard. He came to the end of his driveway, and from a distance of twenty feet, we chatted.

"Man," he said, "this is like living through the slowest sci-fi movie ever."

"It is," I said.

"Yeah," he said, "the world is on pause. It's so creepy. But things will change, we'll be all right."

These days, I've stopped wearing my watch. For the first time in my adult life I don't constantly know what the time is; there are no appointments or errands to tether me to the minute; time has become fluid, like the long blue river we always knew it was. The stepping stones have vanished. It's as if a Taoist master were in charge, giving non-instruction. "There is no path. Surrender to the river."

Still, unused to this degree of turmoil, we try to make sense of what is happening. For me, it's as if the backdrop before which I've always lived my life has instantly become a foreground in which I am negligible. American poet Mary Ruefle also notes this sense of our individual insignificance in her poem "A Late Dense Work":

> *My face a thumbtack*
> *in the earth*

Yet in this newly lived state, this unasked-for awareness, a soft expansion of days is occurring. They're wider, deeper, softer. I've noticed that, and more. Taking a picture this afternoon of a blooming skunk cabbage, I looked closely at the elongated flower, yellow, with a pointed green tip, and at its unfurling outer leaves, which were waxy green. I thought nothing about it, other than what it was, other than to admire it. The same happened with a white rhododendron flower, the way it was peppered on the inside petals with tiny brown dots.

Your directions for killing the spotted-wing drosophila included making a trap out of a plastic container and lid. Punch six holes into the lid, you said, and put an inch of apple cider vinegar in the bottom of the container. Cover the container and set it beside your ravaged strawberry, raspberry, or blueberry plants. Fly death will occur when the flies crawl in after the sweet vinegar. They will either drown or become trapped inside the container.

Yes, I was thinking that too. If only eradicating a virus were this simple.

Meanwhile, spring. The planet turning in spite of us.

We're seeding microgreens beneath a grow light in a downstairs room. Next, a food garden in the backyard. And how ironic this must seem for a person lacking in gardening passion. But the phrase from the last century comes to mind: "Needs must."

And so we will plant, Helen. Calmly, with love.

SOURCES

The opening epigraph is a quote from Tony Hoagland's poem "Real Estate," included in the collection *Priest Turned Therapist Treats Fear of God* (Minneapolis: Greywolf Press, 2018).

#3. Lu Yu (Lù Yǔ 陆羽 / 陸羽). *The Classic of Tea.* Translated by Francis Ross Carpenter. Illustrations by Demi Hitz. Boston: Little, Brown and Company, 1974 [AD 760–762].

#5. Karl Ove Knausgård. *My Struggle.* Books 1–6. New York: Farrar, Strauss and Giroux, 2009–2011.

#7. Jonathan Franzen. "What If We Stopped Pretending?" *New Yorker*, September 8, 2019. www.newyorker.com/culture /cultural-comment/what-if-we-stopped-pretending.

#11. Edith Sitwell. *English Eccentrics: A Gallery of Weird and Wonderful Men and Women.* London, UK: Penguin Books, 1980 [1933].

#12. Paul Valéry's *Notebooks* (1894–1945) are quoted in Charles Simic, *Dime-Store Alchemy: The Art of Joseph Cornell*, New York Review Books Classics series (New York Review of Books, 1992).

#12. The Charles Simic quote is from *The Monster Loves His Laby-rinth: Notebooks* (Port Townsend, WA: Ausable Press, 2008).

#13. Gavin Pretor-Pinney. *The Cloudspotter's Guide: The Science, History, and Culture of Clouds.* London, UK: Hodder & Stoughton, 2006.

#14. I read the Eric Idle paraphrase in an interview somewhere. Between the ages of seven and nineteen, Idle lived in an orphanage: "I had no idea I was going to be ... dumped [at age seven by his mother]. One or two abandonment issues there you can see ..." (IMDb, "Eric Idle: Quotes," m.imdb .com/name/nm0001385/quotes).

#16. Ethan Coen and Joel Coen, dirs. *The Big Lebowski.* Universal City, CA: PolyGram Filmed Entertainment and Gramercy Pictures (Universal Studios), 1988. 117 min.

#18. Eduardo Galeano. *Children of the Days: A Calendar of Human History.* Translated by Mark Fried. New York: Nation Books, 2013.

#20. The William S. Burroughs quote is from James Grauer-holz and Ira Silverberg (eds.), *Word Virus: The William S. Burroughs Reader* (New York: Grove/Atlantic, 2007).

#20. The Gertrude Stein quotes are respectively from *Wars I Have Seen* (London, UK: Brilliance Books, 1984 [1945]) and "On Punctuation" (1935), in *Lectures in America* (Boston: Beacon Press, 1985 [1935]).

#22. Anthony Wing Kosner. "The Mind at Work: Karl Friston on the Brain's Surprising Energy." Part 1 of "The Mind at Work." Dropbox's *Work in Progress* (blog), September 30,

2019. blog.dropbox.com/topics/work-culture/the-mind-at
-work--karl-friston-on-the-brain-s-surprising-energy.

#22. John Hersey. *Hiroshima*. New York: Alfred A. Knopf, 1946. Originally published in *the New Yorker* as its entire issue of August 31, 1946.

#22. The Georgia O'Keefe quote is taken from Fred R. Shapiro (ed.), *The Yale Book of Quotations* (New Haven, CT: Yale University Press, 2006). Originally quoted in the *New York Post*, May 16, 1946.

#22. Greg Jackson. "Vicious Cycles: Theses on a Philosophy of News." *Harper's Magazine*, January 2020.

#22. Cresson H. Kearny. *Nuclear War Survival Skills: Lifesaving Nuclear Facts and Self-Help Instructions.* Oak Ridge, TN: Oak Ridge National Laboratory (U.S. Department of Energy); Coos Bay [Atsixiis], OR: NWS Research Bureau, 1980.

#24. Kurt Vonnegut. *Hocus Pocus*. New York: Berkeley Books, 1990.

#26. Henry David Thoreau. *Walden: or, Life in the Woods; and "Civil Disobedience."* Introduction by W.S. Merwin. Afterword by William Howarth. New York: Signet Classics, 2012 [1854].

#27. Gene Weingarten. *One Day: The Extraordinary Story of an Ordinary 24 Hours in America.* New York: Blue Rider Press, 2019.

#28. The original source of Frank Lloyd Wright's often-quoted phrase – "Study nature, love nature, stay close to nature. It will never fail you" – could not be located.

#29. James Tate. "Roscoe's Farewell." *The Government Lake: Last Poems*. New York: HarperCollins Publishers, 2019.

#33. Phoebe Weston. "'Untold Human Suffering': 11,000 Scientists from across World Unite to Declare Global Climate Emergency." *Independent*, November 5, 2019. www.independent .co.uk/environment/climate-emergency-scientists-emissions -letter-climate-change-a9185786.html.

#33. The Matsuo Bashō (松尾 芭蕉) quote is from *The Narrow Road to the Deep North, and Other Travel Sketches*, trans. Nobuyuki Yuasa, Penguin Classics series (London, UK: Penguin Books, 1966).

#33. Decca Aitkenhead. "James Lovelock: 'Enjoy Life while You Can: In 20 Years Global Warming Will Hit the Fan.'" *Guardian*, March 1, 2008. www.theguardian.com /theguardian/2008/mar/01/scienceofclimatechange .climatechange.

#33. Dan Jason. *Changing the Climate with the Seeds We Sow*. Illustrations by Lyn Alice. Comox, BC: Watershed Sentinel Books, 2020.

#33. Shalu Mehta. "Woman Bringing Holiday Warmth to Those in Need." *Peninsula News Review*, December 11, 2019.

#35. Joseph A. Coannouer. *Weeds: Guardians of the Soil*. Morrisville, NC: Lulu.com, 2015.

#36. The image appearing in letter 36 is in the public domain. It is from René Descartes's 1677 *Tractatus de homine et de formatione fœtus* [Treatise on man and the formation of the fetus] (Amsterdam: Apud Danielem Elsevirium), part 5, pp. 139 and 140. archive.org/details/tractatusdehomino1desc /page/138/mode/2up?.

#38. Elizabeth von Arnim. *Elizabeth and Her German Garden*. New York: Random House, 2001 [1898].

#40. Russell Edson. "With Sincerest Regrets." *The Tunnel: Selected Poems*. Field Poetry Series. Oberlin, OH: Oberlin College Press, 1994.

#44. Kurt Vonnegut. *Man without a Country*. New York: Seven Stories Press, 2005.

#45. Elizabeth von Arnim. *The Solitary Summer*. Boston: Little, Brown and Company, 1993 [1899].

#46. Diana Beresford-Kroeger. *The Sweetness of a Simple Life: Tips for Healthier, Happier and Kinder Living Gleaned from the Wisdom and Science of Nature*. Toronto: Vintage Canada, 2015.

#48. M.A.C. Farrant. "Travel." In *Darwin Alone in the Universe*. Vancouver, BC: Talonbooks, 2003.

#50. The Snowball Earth model is described by Renée Hetherington in a work-in-progress titled *Deep Time*:

> Perhaps, the most remarkable climatic event to occur during Earth's history was episodes of Snowball Earth, when temperatures everywhere dropped below zero for millions of

years causing all surface water on Earth to freeze. The first of three known Snowball Earth episodes happened between about 2.5 and 2.4 billion years ago, when Earth's continents converged around the equator and mid-latitude zones. Earth's atmospheric circulation around tropical regions reversed and a desert formed around the equator. Gradually, snow and ice covered the planet. The accumulating ice and snow reflected light and heat away from Earth's surface, triggering a positive feedback loop that kept cooling the planet and its atmosphere until Earth formed a giant snowball. This first Snowball Earth lasted millions of years until extraordinarily high levels of carbon dioxide in the atmosphere (e.g., 25 to 250 times the current atmospheric levels) interrupted the feedback loop and slipped the plant into a lengthy, warm interval when glaciers and ice sheets stopped forming.

See also Paul F. Hoffman, Dorian S. Abbot, Yosef Ashkenazy, Douglas I. Benn, Jochen J. Brocks, Phoebe A. Cohen, Grant M. Cox, et al., "Snowball Earth Climate Dynamics and Cryogenian Geology-Geobiology," *Science Advances* 3, no. 11 (November 8, 2017), e1600983. doi.org/10.1126/sciadv.1600983.

#52. Deborah Levy. *Things I Don't Want to Know*. London, UK: Penguin Books, 2013.

#52. Deborah Levy. *The Cost of Living*. London, UK: Penguin Books, 2018.

#52. John Gray. *Straw Dogs: Thoughts on Humans and Other Animals*. London, UK: Granta Books, 2003.

#52. Joanna Macy and Molly Young Brown. *Coming Back to Life: The Updated Guide to the Work That Reconnects.* Gabriola Island, BC: New Society Publishers, 2014.

#54. David Markson. *The Last Novel.* Berkeley, CA: Shoemaker & Hoard, 2007.

#56. West Coast Seeds (Mark Macdonald). *2020 Gardening Guide and Seed Catalogue.* viewer.zmags.com /publication/285b6322#/285b6322/1.

#56. Michael Pollan. *The Botany of Desire: A Plant's-Eye View of the World.* New York: Random House, 2001.

#57. Christian Wiman. *My Bright Abyss: Meditation of a Modern Believer.* New York: Farrar, Straus and Giroux, 2013.

#60. Marilyn Kluger. *Preserving Summer's Bounty: A Quick and Easy Guide to Freezing, Canning, Preserving, and Drying What You Grow.* Rodale Garden Books series. New York: M. Evans and Company, 1971.

#60. M.A.C. Farrant. *Girls around the House.* Vancouver, BC: Polestar Book Publishers, 1999.

#64. Mary Ruefle. "A Late Dense Work." In *Dunce.* Seattle, WA: Wave Books, 2019.

ACKNOWLEDGMENTS

My deep thanks to gardening master Helen Chesnut, who graciously allowed me to become, through the writing of this book, her humble adept. Thank you for permission to use your name and your columns in the way that I have. Your practice of "calm abidance" continues to inspire me.

Thank you to Kevin Williams, Vicki Williams, and the Talon team for your support of *One Good Thing*, and, in particular, to Charles Simard who, once again, "saved my (vegan) bacon" during the copy-editing phase. Thank you to andrea bennett for her inspired cover design and accompanying illustrations.

Thank you to Karl Siegler, my long-time editor, for your immeasurable contribution. Your depth of knowledge and experience, and your overarching vision for the book helped me transform the mud of a first draft into a sharper, cleaner version.

Thank you to Mark Macdonald of West Coast Seeds for a convivial conversation about their catalogue.

Love and thanks to: Terry Farrant, Anna Farrant, Bill Farrant, Melanie Ransome, Vicky Husband, Pauline (Jane) Holdstock, Renée Hetherington, Phil Murty, Brett Smyth, and Don Smyth.

M.A.C. Farrant is the award-winning author of seventeen works of fiction, memoirs, and two plays.

She has published eight books with Talonbooks, the most recent being her trio of miniature fiction: *The World Afloat* (2014), *The Days* (2016), and *The Great Happiness* (2019).

She lives in North Saanich, British Columbia.

PHOTO: LAURA SAWCHUK